Representative who shall not have att[ained]

[...] be an Inhabitant of that State in wh[ich]

[... Di]rect Taxes shall be apportioned among [the]

[... determ]ined by adding to the whole Number of [...]

[... othe]r Persons. The actual Enumeration

[... the] Term of ten Years, in such Manner as [...]

[... Sta]te shall have at Least one Representati[ve]

[... Massa]chusetts eight; Rhode Island and Pro[vidence]

[... an]d six; Virginia ten; North Carolina [...]

[... vacancie]s in the Representation from any Sta[te]

[... Represe]ntatives shall chuse their Speaker and [...]

[... of t]he United States shall be composed of t[wo]

[... the]y shall be assembled in Consequence of [...]

[... Seat]s shall be vacated at the Expiration of [...]

[... s]ixth Year, so that one third may be chuse[n]

[... S]tate, the Executive thereof may make tem[porary]

[... S]enator who shall not have attained to [...]

[... Inhabit]ant of that State, for which he shall be [...]

[... the United] States shall be President of the S[enate]

[...] their other Officers, and also a Presiden[t]

TRUTHS

The Future of *America First*

VIVEK RAMASWAMY

THRESHOLD EDITIONS

New York   London   Toronto   Sydney   New Delhi

I dedicate this book to the brave Americans whom I met across the country during my presidential campaign. It was the honor of my life, and the conversations I had with them are what inspired me to write this book.

Threshold Editions
An Imprint of Simon & Schuster, LLC
1230 Avenue of the Americas
New York, NY 10020

First Threshold Editions hardcover edition September 2024

THRESHOLD EDITIONS and colophon are trademarks of Simon & Schuster, LLC

For information about special discounts for bulk purchases, please contact Simon & Schuster Special Sales at 1-866-506-1949 or business@simonandschuster.com.

The Simon & Schuster Speakers Bureau can bring authors to your live event. For more information or to book an event, contact the Simon & Schuster Speakers Bureau at 1-866-248-3049 or visit our website at www.simonspeakers.com.

Manufactured in the United States of America

1   3   5   7   9   10   8   6   4   2

Library of Congress Cataloging-in-Publication Data has been applied for.

ISBN 978-1-6680-7843-3
ISBN 978-1-6680-7845-7 (ebook)

CONTENTS

CONTENTS

PREFACE

What made Donald Trump so compelling as a political leader in the 2016 Republican primary was that, unlike the other candidates, he didn't blindly parrot the party's historical orthodoxy with fancy verbiage. Instead, he offered an entirely new worldview—one that shattered the consensus that had, to that point, pervaded the policy vision of the then-existent Republican Party. He offered a nationalist vision for America's future. He didn't just recite talking points that the rest of the party memorized back in 1980. It's a testament to his success in remaking the Republican Party that what began as a challenge to the old system became the *new* system.

But that raises a new dilemma. We now hear Republican candidates utter phrases by rote like "America-First," "we need to make things here," and "we're the party of the working class"—without actually stopping to ask what these phrases mean, or why exactly we're saying them.

I believe this is not a good development. An important reason why the historical neoliberal consensus failed our country wasn't simply that it failed to predict certain negative consequences of its policy prescriptions. After all, no political or economic theory is ever perfect.

Rather, the deeper problem with the old neoliberal consensus was the intellectual laziness and capture through which it earned its staying power. Even after the 2008 financial crisis, the neoliberal consensus on immigration, trade, and foreign policy became so codified as dogma in the Republican Party that our presidential nominees like John McCain and Mitt Romney didn't know exactly why they were saying the things they were saying. All they knew is that they were supposed to say it.

The America First movement must be careful to avoid that mistake. Right now, the movement's most important objective is to reelect Trump, but there's a deeper question that is less urgent, yet no less important— where this movement goes after a successful second Trump term. That's what this book is really about.

I see two distinct possibilities. Let's call the first "National Patronage," and the second "National Liberty." Both are unapologetically nationalist. Both reject the old neoliberal consensus on foreign policy, trade, and immigration—but have very different proposals for future policy.

The current National Patronage consensus is that we need less international trade altogether; that we should use tariffs to stop other countries (including, but not limited to, China) from flooding our markets; and that government should use taxpayer resources to purposefully subsidize critical areas of American production where we are less competitive today. By contrast, the National Liberty objective is to eliminate U.S. dependence on China in critical areas for U.S. security. That necessarily means more—not less—U.S. trade with allies like Japan and South Korea, India and the Philippines, who can fill the void left by cutting the cord from China in areas like pharmaceutical supply chains and our own military industrial base.

To the National Liberty wing, the top objectives of U.S. immigration policy are: protecting U.S. national security, preserving U.S. national identity, and promoting U.S. economic growth—*in that order*. That's different from the myopic neoliberal worldview that promoted economic growth even at the expense of national security and national identity. But it's also different from the National Patronage camp, which promotes protecting the wages of American workers even at the expense of other important national objectives.

The National Patronage camp believes in reshaping and redirecting the regulatory state to advance policies that improve the plight of American workers and manufacturers. By contrast, the National Liberty camp believes the only way to improve the plight of America, including our workers and manufacturers, isn't by reinventing the regulatory state—but by *dismantling* the regulatory state.

This intellectual debate—on trade, legal immigration, and especially the regulatory state—will be the defining rift in the future of the conservative movement. The chasm is seismic, not slight. But for now it lurks beneath the surface, against the backdrop of a looming presidential election.

Regardless of which camp prevails, the movement will be stronger if we understand these rifts rather than pretend they don't exist, and build on the common ground between the two.

INTRODUCTION

Say what you will about the modern left, they're very good at articulating a coherent vision for humanity. They believe our relationships to one another are defined by power dynamics. Just as predators wield power over prey in the wild, oppressors wield power over the oppressed in civil society. The old left defined power based on wealth; the new left defines it based on race, gender, and sexuality. The role of government is to rectify these injustices from the state of nature.

Whether this account of human relations is *true* is of less concern to them than whether it's a coherent narrative to motivate action.

And they are exceptional at cultivating urgency to act. These power imbalances must be corrected before a fixed deadline—say, the pending destruction of humanity due to global cooling (in the 1970s), or the pending destruction of humanity due to global warming (in the post-2000s), or the pending destruction of humanity due to Covid-19 (in 2020). Staving off such catastrophes requires enlightened elites to work together across national boundaries for the greater global good.

As conservatives, we know we're against *that*. We're anti-woke. We're anti-globalist. We're anti–big government. We know what we stand *against*. But what exactly do we stand for?

The fact that this is a hard question to answer is a damning indictment of the modern Republican Party, which has abjectly failed to articulate an affirmative alternative to the left's vision. This represents an inexcusable dereliction of duty. Relentlessly criticizing the hypocrisies of the other side will get us only so far. Fighting against someone is different from fighting for your own cause.

This is no longer a theoretical matter. Despite lofty expectations and self-congratulatory rhetoric, Republicans delivered abysmal results at the ballot box in 2018, 2020, 2022, and 2023. Various factions of the party blamed one-off things ranging from abortion to Donald Trump for these failures, but the real reason is far more basic: we lack a positive alternative to the left's vision for the future. The Republican message in 2022 was to rail against "the radical Biden agenda," and it didn't work: the long-predicted red wave never came. As this book goes to print, I worry about a similar outcome in 2024, unless we muster the courage to define who we really are as conservatives.

So what exactly do we stand *for*? This book offers an answer to that question: we stand for truth. The modern left has abandoned truth, often dismissing it as an inconvenient social construct. Consider the words of Katherine Maher, the new CEO of National Public Radio: "For our most tricky disagreements, seeking the truth and seeking to convince others of the truth might not be the right place to start. In fact, our reverence for the truth might be a distraction that's getting in the way of finding common ground and getting things done."[1] I reject that view. Truth isn't relative. It isn't dispensable. It isn't an inconvenience. It's vital. It's the only thing that matters in the end. The truth is what sets us free.

In the pages ahead, I lay out ten hard truths that the American conservative movement must embrace wholeheartedly if we are to stand a chance of saving our nation before we permanently lose it. If this book were published back when I was in high school in the early 2000s, I would have advised you to save your money because these truths were too obvious. Today, I'd caution you to make sure you're ready for the consequences of publicly repeating anything you're about to read. Just last year, a small group of vocal activists tried to publicly oust me from the board of my high school alma mater, for committing the high crime of stating several truths you will encounter. These statements have turned me into a persona non grata across much of corporate America, where countless companies would have otherwise been thrilled to have me on their boards. But if I learned one thing from my presidential campaign, it's this: your convictions mean nothing unless you're willing to sacrifice to defend them.

We'll examine truths spanning an unusually broad range of matters—from the biological basis for two genders, to the untold positive effects of warmer global surface temperatures, to the origin of Covid-19 and what modern quantum physics suggests about the existence of God. We'll explore policy proposals that fall outside the Overton Window of both major parties, from eliminating birthright citizenship for the kids of illegal immigrants to requiring civics exams and loyalty oaths for high school graduates as a precondition for full citizenship.

Each of the ten subject areas in this book deserves its own book-length treatment. Indeed I draw from the life's work of many scholars who have dedicated themselves to the topics we are about to cover. But this book isn't an academic exposition. Instead, it is designed to arm you with the right arguments for friendly debates at the dinner table. Each chapter ends with five short points that you can take to the next contentious conversation that you have with a left-leaning friend, colleague, or family member. I believe that's how we will save our nation. Not through self-censorship, but through open conversation. Not by preaching to those who already agree with us, but by sincerely engaging with those who don't. Not through violence, but through hard debate.

That's the America I know, the America I miss—a nation where you can vehemently disagree with your neighbor about politics while still loving and respecting him in the end, so much so that you can freely tell him what you *actually* think, instead of projecting an artifice you believe he can "handle." A nation where our relationships with our fellow citizens start in workplaces and on the baseball field, in the living room and at block parties, so far from the domain of partisan politics that when we *do* from time to time inevitably end up in heated confrontations, we know that we begin from a common place in pursuit of shared truth, rather than from irreconcilable starting points.

When even the mundane becomes controversial, our nation suffers. The best way to solve a problem is to name it first. So let's speak the truth without fear and see what happens. I'll do my part in the pages ahead, and after that I'm counting on you to join me.

1

GOD IS REAL

In the spring of 2023, during the early stages of my presidential campaign, I took a short break on one of my innumerable flights across country to spend some quality time with my most frequent travel companion: a vinyl-bound black notebook that slipped easily into my backpack. At the time, the book was filled with a potpourri of mundane to-do lists and free-flowing reflections of my experiences on the campaign trail. That day, I decided to take a few minutes to write down a handful of things that I knew to be *true*.

It didn't take long for me to jot down the first truth on the list: *God is real*. I took another twenty minutes or so to write out another nine: there are two genders; human prosperity requires fossil fuels; reverse racism is racism; an open border is not a border; parents should determine the education of their children; the nuclear family is the greatest form of governance known to man; capitalism lifts people up from poverty; there are three branches of U.S. government; and the U.S. Constitution is the strongest guarantor of freedom in human history.

There are countless other true statements I *could* have written down but chose not to—for example, that the earth revolves around the sun. Most everyone knows that fact to be true, and therefore there would be nary any dissent if you decided to say so in public—at least not in the year

2023. Of course, back in 1633, it *did* land Galileo under house arrest for heresy until his death.

I was looking for obvious truths that were as contested in 2023 as Galileo's heliocentrism had been in 1633. All ten statements would have been banal just twenty years ago and hopefully, even a few years from now, they will be once again. But in 2023, they felt somewhat heretical, which is what compelled me to say them so emphatically.

Obvious yet controversial is a rare but powerful combination. It brings political audiences to their feet like electricity lighting up a sleepy room. Writing down those ten truths was arguably the most important inflection point in my campaign.

It was odd. I received standing ovations in the middle of countless speeches just for stating simple things that most people knew to be true. On more than one occasion, I had to end a lengthy preplanned speech on the spot—because there was nothing more I could say to top the din of an audience that was on its feet in the middle of my speech.

It was usually the first "truth" that woke the crowd up: *God is real*. It was provocative. It was pithy. And it was *true*.

No doubt people were surprised to hear it from *me*. After all, one of the first things most voters knew about me was that I was not a Christian. Fewer of them knew that I'd been raised in the Vedanta tradition of the Hindu religion, which is far closer to Christianity than most people assume. Since childhood, I've been raised with the idea that there is one God of whom there are multiple different forms, not multiple Gods. Throughout the campaign, I would often be approached by people who didn't understand this. I'd also be attacked by other candidates (or, more precisely, their super PACs) who saw my faith as a weakness. But the main point never changed.

It still hasn't.

Our nation was founded on the principle that God is real. For many years, we stuck to this principle, mentioning God during our ceremonies and referring to Him when making important decisions as a community or as a nation. To be sure, it's not the proper role of government to establish any one religion, and part of what makes America great is that we respect citizens who believe in God equally to those who don't. I'm not advocating *government* favoritism toward any one faith, or even religion at all. The beautiful thing about the United States is that people are free not to believe in God and still enjoy all the freedoms that religious people have. The government should not foist religion onto anyone. Rather I'm concerned about a newly emergent *cultural* hostility against people of faith. Only recently has the notion of God—especially in the public square—fallen out of favor, especially among the kinds of people I encountered at Harvard, Yale, and various social circles in Silicon Valley. To these people, belief in God is a relic of a bygone age, and we should work every day to move beyond it.

For the most part, these people believe they have truth—better known as "the science"—on their side. They cite things like the big bang or the theory of evolution to prove that God could not possibly have created the world and human beings. Most secular atheists I know are good people, but that doesn't make the institutionalization of their beliefs good for our nation. Indeed atheism has become the de facto position for most intellectuals in this country.

This is a bad development, and not just because atheism has led to untold misery for millions of people throughout history, from the French Revolution to the communist dictatorships of the twentieth century. Our culture's turn away from God is unfortunate because it is a turn away from truth—and an abandonment of one of America's founding convictions.

"SCIENCE DISPROVES THE EXISTENCE OF GOD"

In the opening scene of Cixin Liu's novel *The Three-Body Problem*, recently adapted by Netflix, a physics professor is brought out onto a stage in front of thousands of young people. The setting is China in the late 1960s. The professor is accused of being a "reactionary," meaning he holds ideas that go against the Marxist regime of Mao Zedong.

A soldier asks the professor if he has taught his students about the big bang. He says yes, noting that it is "currently the most plausible explanation for the origin of the universe." The soldier beats him, calling his words "lies."

"The theory," says the soldier, "leaves open a place to be filled by God."

The events of this novel are fictional, but the scenes it portrays are based very much on real life. All over China in the middle of the twentieth century, the government held "struggle sessions," attempting to beat ideas they didn't like out of people. Surprisingly, one of the ideas it hated the most was the big bang, which contradicted notions of the infinity and eternity of matter, both of which were crucial to the dialectical materialism of Russian revolutionary Vladimir Lenin.

In fact, when the big bang emerged as a theory in the early twentieth century, the Catholic Church was thrilled. Speaking at a conference in the Vatican in 1951, Pope Pius XII said that the big bang "bore witness to that primordial *Fiat lux* uttered at the moment when, along with matter, there burst forth from nothing a sea of light and radiation. . . . Hence, creation took place in time, therefore there is a creator, therefore God exists!"

It might surprise you to learn that the Catholic Church reacted with joy when the theory of the big bang was first introduced. It might also surprise you to learn that the man who first discovered it, Georges Lemaître, was a Catholic priest.

For years now, in the wake of the New Atheist movement and stunning advances in our knowledge about the universe, it's tempting to believe that we have a complete picture of the origins of our universe and how it works.

We don't.

In fact, as the physicist Steven Weinberg noted in a 2008 essay, "As we make progress understanding the expanding universe, the problem itself expands, so that the solution always seems to recede from us."[1] Recently, the physicist (and committed atheist) Lawrence Krauss has written an excellent book called *The Edge of Knowledge*, enumerating all the things we still don't understand. Among the questions he tackles: "How did our universe begin, if it even had a beginning? How will it end? How big is it? What lies beyond what we can see? What are the fundamental laws governing our existence? Are those laws the same everywhere? What is the world of our experience made of? What remains hidden? How did life on earth arise? Are we alone? What is consciousness? Is human consciousness unique?"[2]

The answer to all these questions: *We don't know.*

At present, the things we don't know about the universe greatly outnumber the things we do know, and like the universe, the number of things we don't know is expanding every day. We don't know, to take just one example, which of our models for understanding the universe is correct. The first model, which most kids who take high school physics learn, is special relativity, best exemplified by Albert Einstein's famous equation $E = MC^2$. According to special relativity, which is, at heart, a theory of "how speed affects mass, time, and space," objects act upon one another in clearly observable ways. Actions have local causes that we can study.

In the latter half of the twentieth century, another theory emerged, this one dealing with more microscopic elements of our universe. It is called quantum mechanics, and it rests on a principle that Einstein dubbed "spooky action." In quantum mechanics, when two particles are "quantum entangled," a change in one will instantaneously effect a change in the other, no matter where in the universe they are placed.

As the science writer Corey Powell put it in 2015, this problem represents "a clash of genuinely incompatible descriptions of reality."[3]

Over the years, proponents of something called string theory have attempted to reconcile the two visions of the universe, with little success. Recently, the Columbia University physicist Peter Woit has made a convincing case that the whole project of string theory is flawed—that the theory "has become a degenerative research project" that is "increasingly complicated and, at the same time, removed from empirical reality."[4]

To be clear, I'm not a physicist. I won't make any claims here about the validity of different theories about how our universe operates, at least not at the technical level. But anyone who looks closely at the scientific literature on big questions about the universe will soon find that things are getting *more* complicated, not less. Contradictions arise every day among competing theories about where the universe came from, where it's going, and even how it's operating at this very moment.

And even if we did understand all the precise machinations of our universe, we still wouldn't have answered the most important question, which is, in effect: *Why?*

All science can do is *describe* the universe. To assume it can explain why the universe exists in the first place is, to quote the writer and podcast host Alex O'Connor, "a category error." During a recent debate for the website UnHerd, O'Connor (another committed atheist) gave one of the best illustrations of this category error that I've heard—one that reflects many centuries of deep thought on the subject.

Suppose, he says, you come across a book of William Shakespeare's sonnets while walking in the woods one day. In your world, Shakespeare does not exist; neither does poetry. So you begin studying this strange object, trying to find out where it comes from. After a while, you manage to figure out that the lines have a rhythm when spoken aloud, which you call "the law of iambic pentameter." You notice that there are small dots at the ends of the sentences, which seem to indicate the conclusions of thoughts. You call this "the law of periods." Yet even after all this, when someone asks you where the book came from, you'll still have to admit that you don't know.

Studying the final product, in other words, gives you little insight into why that final product is there in the first place.

We can, however, reliably rule out the assumption favored by most modern scientists, which is that the universe simply appeared out of nothing for no reason. In a sense, this would be as absurd as thinking that a book of Shakespeare's sonnets simply assembled itself—that trees fell and assembled themselves into paper, and globules of ink arranged themselves into lines of poetry. It turns out that the analogy to poetry is more apt than most people realize. In our universe, everything—from the smallest particles to the forces that govern all objects—seems "fine-tuned," to borrow a phrase from the physicist Paul Davies, for life.

In the book *God: The Evidence*, the writer Patrick Glynn gives just a few of the amazing coincidences that physics cannot explain:

- A stronger nuclear strong force (by as little as 2 percent) would have prevented the formation of protons—yielding a universe without atoms. Decreasing it by 5 percent would have given us a universe without stars.
- The very nature of water—so vital to life—is something of a mystery (a point noticed by one of the forerunners of anthropic reasoning in the nineteenth century, Harvard biologist Lawrence Henderson). Unique among the molecules, water is lighter in its solid than liquid form: Ice floats. If it did not, the oceans would freeze from the bottom up and earth would now be covered with solid ice. This property in turn is traceable to unique properties of the hydrogen atom.

"The list," as Glynn writes, "goes on."

The more we dig in, the more it seems that Aristotle was correct when he posited the existence of an "unmoved mover" who started the universe. In fact, while many thinkers throughout history—Thomas Jefferson among them—have quibbled with specific principles of theism (meaning, in its broadest sense, the notion that God intervenes in human affairs), very few have been able to produce credible evidence against Deism (the notion that the universe has a definite beginning, namely God).

The point is not that science proves the existence of God. It doesn't. And it probably can't. Rather, the point is that science has not—and cannot—*disprove* the existence of God, nor can it explain the moral sense with which we are all instilled at birth. Yet this still leaves the issue of religion on the table. Why, many opponents of religion wonder, do we still cling to religion as a source of morality and community? Can't that all be replaced by more modern ideals like secular humanism?

The answer, I believe, is no.

THE UNANSWERED MYSTERY OF UNIVERSAL MORALITY

In the late 1780s, when the United States of America was only a few years old, a German philosopher named Immanuel Kant began writing his masterwork, *Critique of Practical Reason*. In this book, which would go on to break the brains of many undergraduate students of philosophy (me included), Kant writes, "Two things fill the mind with ever new and increasing admiration and awe, the oftener and the more steadily we reflect on them: the starry heavens above and the moral law within."

Most people don't have trouble understanding the first part. After all, who hasn't looked up at the night sky in wonder and asked questions about where it all came from, how far out it goes, and how long it will be here? It's almost impossible not to feel some sense of wonder when contemplating the intricacies of the universe, as we just did for a few pages.

The second part is less obvious, although I (as well as many great thinkers throughout history) would argue that it's just as important. How, you might wonder, do we get our sense of what is right and what is wrong? What is love, and where does it come from? Today, it's common to believe that these things are innate in us, no different than hair color or eye color.

Some modern thinkers, the writer and neuroscientist Sam Harris among them, believe that morality comes down to neurons firing in our brains, and that there is nothing otherworldly or divine about it.

In his book *The Moral Landscape*, he writes, "Values . . . translate into facts that can be scientifically understood: regarding positive and negative social emotions, retributive impulses, the effects of specific laws and social institutions on human relationships, the neurophysiology of happiness and suffering, etc."

This might well be true. But we are still left with the question of where morality comes from in the first place. For atheists, this isn't an important question. To them, human beings are simply sacks of meat whose actions are the product of molecules in motion; there is no divine hand at work at any point in the process. It's no wonder that so many of them, Harris included, have come to believe that free will as a concept does not exist. How could you believe anything else when your worldview leaves no place for God?

Like most people, I am fascinated by the "moral law" within me. Take a second to think about it, and I'm sure you will be too. When I contemplate my sense of right and wrong—or my hardwired notions of a universal good, which I drive toward while making decisions—I feel the presence of something other than neurons firing in my brain.

I'm probably not alone. Everyone—Christian, Muslim, theist, atheist—is imbued with an intrinsic sense of morality and fairness; to paraphrase the inimitable humorist David Wong, we all live as if the absolute morality of some supreme lawmaker were true.[5]

When someone steals from us, we don't just say "ah, that person is exhibiting social deviance"—we're mad. We want *justice*. When a husband cheats, we feel betrayed. Hurt. Violated. We know right from wrong, and we know it because it is instilled in us by God.

The social science confirms that morality is universal and innate. Monkeys that are rewarded with cucumbers will continue to plow along performing tasks for a researcher happily enough.[6] But give one monkey grapes—a much-preferred treat—and the others will revolt, occasionally throwing their once-treasured cucumbers out of the cage. They understand that the situation is inherently unfair.

It's not just a matter of self-interest; we have an innate sense of morality even when we have nothing personally at stake. One clever study examined infants just eight months old.[7] Babies can't speak, of course, so the researchers got creative. They designed a videogame involving anthropomorphic blocks with eyes on them. The babies wore gear that tracked where they were looking. When the babies stared at a single block too long, a square without eyes would fall from the top of the screen, crushing it. If the babies moved their eyes around enough, no blocks were destroyed. Once the babies understood the controls, the researchers introduced a new variable: blocks harming one another. More precisely, the babies watched one of the humanized blocks colliding with and pushing another humanized block against the side of the screen. After witnessing this block-on-block harassment, 75 percent of babies gave the aggressor block the literal death stare. We are all born with a moral impulse, with a fundamental sense of what is good and bad, kind and unkind, ethical and unethical.

Throughout history, great thinkers have asked why this might be.

For Kant, whose words opened this section, the presence of a moral law within all of us, which he called the "categorical imperative," compels people to act according to principles that could be universally applied. For Kant, the existence of this moral law implied the necessity of a kind of moral legislator, a being who enforces the moral order. Without God, moral law would lack ultimate purpose and coherence, reducing moral duties to mere subjective preferences rather than objective truths. Only a higher power, in his eyes, could ensure that moral virtue is ultimately rewarded, aligning with the highest good, which Kant defines as the union of happiness and virtue. Thus, Kant concludes that the postulation of God is a "moral necessity" to make sense of the moral law that we inherently recognize and strive to follow.

Of course, the lines of reasoning found in Kant are complex, and they only get more complex the deeper you dig.

Luckily, similar lines of reasoning can be found elsewhere, written in far more modern, easily digestible prose. In his book *Mere Christianity*, the writer C. S. Lewis—known to children everywhere as the author of the Chronicles of Narnia books—details the journey he took from atheism to Christianity, building on Kant's ideas about moral laws. In the beginning, he writes, the horrible things he saw all around him made him believe that God could not possibly exist; how, he wondered, was it possible for such evil to exist in a universe created by a being who was supposedly all-knowing and all-loving?

The change came when he realized that his belief in right and wrong—the very thing that allowed him to realize that our universe *was*, in fact, flawed—was most likely the result of divine origin.

"A man does not call a line crooked," he writes in *Mere Christianity*, "unless he has some idea of a straight line."

In other words, our conception of the good must come from something outside our biology. Our senses of justice, fairness, and duty point to a higher standard beyond human invention. There is no good reason to assume that ideas about a universal morality—which have held more or less constant throughout the ages, and across many cultures—could have come during the process of Darwinian evolution. The argument has been put it in its simplest form by the philosopher William Lane Craig, who often says, "If God does not exist, objective moral values do not exist; objective moral values do exist; therefore, God exists."

TRUTH AND LOVE

If that seems too neat, consider that your senses might not be quite as reliable as you think. In what is perhaps the most complicated (and compelling) moral argument for the existence of God, the philosopher Alvin

Plantinga has put forth something known as the "Evolutionary Argument Against Naturalism." According to this argument, the cognitive faculties of human beings have evolved according to the laws of Darwinian evolution, which favors traits that enhance survival and reproduction, but not necessarily those that lead to true beliefs. So, it follows that if our brains are shaped by evolution, they are geared not toward finding truth, but surviving. This means that our rational faculties—the ones that atheists believe we use to come up with our moral laws—cannot be relied upon to produce *anything*, let alone complex laws that govern our every action. Naturalism, therefore, is false, and some form of supernaturalism (belief in God, for instance) must be the foundation for rational cognition.

During the research for this chapter, I've come across several complex ideas like this one, all of which make convincing cases for the existence of a higher power. To address them all at length here would take the rest of the book—and we have plenty of other "truths" to consider. But it's worth mentioning that there is one other common argument for the existence of God, and it is far simpler than the rest.

Love, according to some modern philosophers, is proof enough that human beings are made of more than just matter. It makes sense. After all, true love often involves self-sacrifice and putting others ahead of ourselves. As the modern philosopher Tim Keller has put it in his book *Reasons for God*, "If we are merely a product of evolution, then there is no reason to put others ahead of ourselves." Yet we put others ahead of ourselves all the time. We act in ways that are inexplicable under an evolutionary framework, and we often do so because of love. To many thinkers, C. S. Lewis among them, this points to a divine origin for our feelings of love.

Evolutionary theory could plausibly explain my unconditional love for my two sons, Karthik and Arjun—and the fact that I would do anything for their well-being and protection, including to sacrifice my life if necessary—because I care about the propagation of my genes. But the Darwinian account decidedly *cannot* explain why I would do the same for my wife, Apoorva, or why my own father would do the same for my mother until their end of days. Darwinism just can't explain selfless unconditional love on earth, for the same reason it ignores the possibility of the divine—not because Darwinism is wrong, but because it's limited in the scope of what it can possibly explain.

In any case, this entire discussion about Darwinism misses the point of what faith is really about. Faith is the conviction that there is a higher power looking after us, taking care of us, guiding us to do the right thing and to bring up those around us. It's the conviction that even if I were to stop believing in that higher power, He won't stop believing in me.

The truth is that I didn't particularly believe in God in my early twenties. What eventually convinced me wasn't an article or a book, just as this chapter likely won't convince many nonbelievers either. It was my experience of falling in love with Apoorva. I didn't just feel like a "lucky guy" to meet her; it felt like *destiny*. Every time I looked into her eyes at the end of a long dinner, or even at the end of a contentious fight, or lay beside her in bed on a lazy Saturday morning, I knew there was no universe in which her soul and mine weren't fated to be joined.

In a universe *without* God, could I have met some other beautiful woman with whom I could go on to procreate and live a satisfactory life? Sure, that's the stochastic world that an evolutionary theorist envisions. But my experience of faith is to know that no such other universe exists. I knew that a higher power guided me to the love of my life, with whom I was meant to form this beautiful family, and it couldn't have been any other way. God has given each of us—myself, Apoorva, our two sons—incredible gifts, and with that we have responsibilities, a duty to fulfill by nature of the blessings we have been given. Apoorva and I were *meant* to bring our sons into this world and they will go on to do God's work. That's not a scientific claim. That's *faith*.

That's what more children and young people need—that certainty that someone loves them and wants them to fulfill their potential, that they are given unique gifts by God that they can use to serve themselves and those around them, that God has a plan for us and is working *through* us to realize it. There is no better antidote for the nihilistic ennui that pervades our country today. Go to a college campus and see a generation, depressed, searching for meaning. Go *anywhere* in our country and see a society searching for meaning. There's more to life than the aimless passage of time, iPhones, and antidepressants. We need only open our eyes to see it.

WHAT FAITH GIVES US

During a recent interview with a radio program in Britain, the evolutionary biologist Richard Dawkins shocked the world by proclaiming that although he didn't believe a word of the Christian faith, he did consider himself "a cultural Christian."

As he put it, "I'm not one of those who wants to stop Christian traditions. This is historically a Christian country. I'm a cultural Christian. . . . So, yes, I like singing carols along with everybody else. I'm not one of those who wants to purge our society of our Christian history."[8]

For years, Dawkins has been one of the loudest voices in the new atheist movement, along with Sam Harris, the late Christopher Hitchens, and many other well-known philosophers. He has celebrated the decline of Christianity in the West, denouncing belief in God as a "delusion" and "superstition."

The reason for his sudden change of heart seems to stem from a worry about what might replace Christianity if it ever went away—a worry that has become increasingly important with the rise of forces such as militant Islam and wokeness, both of which pose unique threats to Western society. As Dawkins himself put it in a tweet from 2018, "Before we rejoice at the death throes of the relatively benign Christian religion, let's not forget Hilaire Belloc's menacing rhyme: 'Always keep a-hold of nurse / For fear of finding something worse.'"[9]

The tweet, which linked to a study showing that 70 percent of young people in the United Kingdom identified as having "no religion," points to an important truth, namely that humans are hardwired for belief in *something*. And when the belief system that has sustained and nourished millions in the West for centuries, which can broadly be called Judeo-Christianity, disappears, any number of things can rise and fill the vacuum.

None of them are good.

Throughout history, we find countless examples of the chaos and depravity that emerges whenever societies attempt to throw off religion permanently. The French Revolution, with its Reign of Terror, sought to replace the Catholic Church with a state-sponsored Cult of Reason, leading to widespread violence and tyranny. In Mao's China, the Cultural Revolution aimed to eradicate traditional beliefs and practices, resulting in immense suffering and the persecution of millions. Similarly, the Soviet Union's aggressive atheism under Joseph Stalin fostered an environment of repression and fear, where dissenters were brutally silenced.

Today, as the writer Ayan Hirsi Ali has recently observed in a piece about her conversion to Christianity, we are under threat from "different but related forces: the resurgence of great-power authoritarianism and expansionism in the forms of the Chinese Communist Party and Vladimir Putin's Russia; the rise of global Islamism, which threatens to mobilise a vast population against the West; and the viral spread of woke ideology, which is eating into the moral fibre of the next generation."[10]

Against these forces, she writes, we must look to what unites us. And what unites us, in her view—which I share—is the legacy of the Judeo-Christian tradition, which can be defined broadly as "an elaborate set of ideas and institutions designed to safeguard human life, freedom and dignity—from the nation state and the rule of law to the institutions of science, health, and learning."[11]

FOUNDATIONS

Whether you buy these arguments or not, it is beyond doubt that the Founders of the United States *did* believe in God, and that the idea of the divine was immensely important to their vision for the country. Like it or not, our nation was founded on these principles—and, by extension, on the premise that God is real. As legal scholars Michael McConnell and Nathan Chapman write in their book *Agreeing to Disagree*, the Founders understood that freedom of conscience, including the free exercise of religious beliefs, was a critical component of liberty. The Founders knew first-hand what establishment of religion looked like, as many early Americans had fled the Crown to escape precisely that tyranny. At the same time, the Founders also understood that religious institutions were an integral part of a well-functioning democracy, as religion laid the groundwork for morality and civility, without which self-governance could not survive.

As Jefferson wrote, "Can the liberties of a nation be thought secure when we have removed their only firm basis, a conviction in the minds of the people that these liberties are a gift of God?" John Adams, a member of the opposing political party back then, agreed: "We have no government armed with power capable of contending with human passions unbridled by morality and religion. . . . Our Constitution was made for a moral and religious people."

George Washington echoed these sentiments, and made the point—widely accepted at the time—that morality alone would not suffice to sustain the fledgling republic: "Let us with caution indulge the supposition that morality can be maintained without religion. Whatever may be conceded to the influence of refined education on minds of peculiar structure, reason and experience forbid us to expect that national morality can prevail in exclusion of religious principle."

As Alexis de Tocqueville would write in the 1830s, "Despotism may be able to do without faith, but freedom cannot. Religion is much more needed in the republic they advocate than in the monarchy they attack, and in democratic republics, most of all. How could society escape destruction if, when political ties are relaxed, moral ties are not tightened?"

Indeed, religion was thought to be so important to the success of the new republic that it is enshrined in our Constitution twice, in both the Establishment Clause and the Free Exercise Clause. Today these clauses are commonly misunderstood as intending to protect the government from the dangerous and unsavory effects of religion. "The separation of church and state" is the common saying, and many people think the goal is to build a wall between the two, to secularize our government. But our Founders had the exact opposite idea in mind. They knew how critical religion was to the proper functioning of a democratic government, and so wanted to protect religious institutions from government interference.

But just as steadfast as our Founders' commitment to religious pluralism and freedom—including the freedom to be atheist—was their conviction that the United States of America is itself still one nation under God. If we cancel that part of our national narrative, we risk canceling some of the most important parts of the rest too.

Our Founders needed to believe in something bigger than themselves to spawn a great nation. And we must too if we are to preserve it. Secular humanism may work for a good number of people in guiding them through living a moral life, while finding sufficient individual purpose and meaning. But it's insufficient at the level of a nation—certainly a nation founded on the idea that we are endowed by our Creator with inalienable rights. Without a critical mass of people in the United States reembracing faith in God—a higher being greater than themselves—I am skeptical that we can fully reverse what so many Americans have accepted as our inevitable national decline.

I remember attending a sermon of a different pastor in Iowa who taught that to be a true Christian, you can't just vaguely believe in the "philosophical teachings of Jesus Christ" (as, say, Jefferson did), but that you had to believe that Jesus Christ was actually *right* about what he said—that he was the sole son of God, and that the path to Truth runs exclusively through him. "Either he was a crazy man, or he was right . . . you can't believe both," the pastor said.

Well, I'd say something similar of our Founding Fathers. If you are truly committed to reviving the 1776 ideals on which our nation was built, either you believe in those founding ideals or you don't. Rejecting Divine Providence while accepting the ideals bequeathed by our Founders who believed in a higher power that created those rights isn't a coherent position.

This brings me back to Richard Dawkins, who seems to believe that modern people can enjoy fundamentally Christian things such as Christmas, universal human rights, and the sight of wonderful cathedrals *without* the beliefs that brought those things into being in the first place. Without believing Christians, there can be no "cultural Christianity."

Fortunately, the problem of religious decline is not quite as drastic in the United States as it is in Europe. According to a Gallup poll taken in 2022, 81 percent of Americans answered "yes" when asked whether they believe in God. So, the real risk we face today is the one that our Founders didn't quite envision—not a tyranny of the majority, but instead a tyranny of the minority. Every day, this vocal minority attempts to enforce a strange set of new ideas—which, as several thinkers have pointed out, functions essentially as a replacement religion—and threaten with social ostracism anyone who dares to disagree.

As even the devout atheist Dawkins has pointed out recently, we must be very careful with how quickly we allow religious tenets to seep out of our public life. What replaces those tenets—specifically from the radical left—will almost certainly end up being much worse, if only because adherents of the new far-left religion believe in their cause with at least as much fervor as any religious fundamentalists we've ever seen.

If you don't believe me, turn the page.

FIVE TRUTHS

1. Believing in science and believing in God are not contradictory but compatible: it's no coincidence that many of the greatest scientists in history believed in God.

2. The big bang theory is consistent with, and even affirms, the concept of a Creator because it suggests a definitive moment of creation from nothing.

3. The fact that human beings across time and space share inherent concepts of right and wrong supports the idea that our ethical instincts are grounded in higher truth.

4. Regardless of whether you believe in God, it's a fact that the founding of the United States was deeply intertwined with our Founders' conviction in a higher power, which influenced the governance and societal structure of our nation.

5. Reviving faith in God—or at least fostering respect rather than disdain for those who believe in God—would reduce division and realign the United States of America with our founding ideals.

2

THE CLIMATE CHANGE AGENDA IS A HOAX

The stadium was packed in Milwaukee for the first Republican primary debate, and about thirty minutes into the debate, the first question came in via video stream: what are you going to do as U.S. president to address the climate crisis?

At first, I was certain I'd misheard the question. This was a *Republican* presidential primary.

But it was soon confirmed that I'd heard correctly indeed. One of the debate moderators asked everyone onstage the same question: *Raise your hand if you acknowledge that human behavior is causing climate change.*

Ron DeSantis stood to my right, both of us center-stage, in front of a silent audience. In my peripheral vision, I saw him start to fidget, and then he suddenly blurted into the microphone a plea to the moderator that we should actually "have the debate" instead of raising our hands like schoolchildren.

That was a well-known trick in the arsenal of presidential debate prep. Every candidate gets coached on the old adage that if you don't want to answer a question, turn it back on the moderator. Donald Trump executed it masterfully in his 2016 run, but it turns out Ron's attempt to do the same fell flat as a naked attempt to avoid the question.

So I decided to call it out: "I'm the only candidate onstage who isn't bought and paid for, so I can say this: the climate change agenda is a hoax."[1]

Shock rippled through the stadium. The press panned me afterward. Donors called to tell me that my response to that question alone caused me to lose credibility with them, and a few gently encouraged me to walk back my position in future interviews.

But I stand by what I said about climate change and here's why: the climate change agenda is a hoax *because it has nothing to do with the climate.* The question of whether man-made climate change is "real" is the wrong question. And that's the heart of the hoax.

Climate change activists argue that global surface temperatures are rising at a worrisome rate due to man-made carbon dioxide emissions, and that we must alter human behaviors to emit less carbon dioxide or else we risk the future of humanity and our planet. That argument purposefully elides the distinction between at least four distinct questions.

Let's examine each in turn.

ARE GLOBAL SURFACE TEMPERATURES RISING?

This is an empirical question, not a philosophical one. The answer appears to be yes, though less definitively than you'd expect based on what you read in the mainstream and even scientific press. In the 1970s, climate change activists were concerned not about global warming—but about global *cooling.* The magazine covers of *Newsweek* and *Time* contained images of large expanses of land covered in glaciers and warned that absent meaningful changes in human behavior, humanity would be at risk of freezing itself to extinction. They pointed to multiyear evidence suggesting that global surface temperatures were declining, and that these declines in surface temperatures appeared to correlate with human impact on the environment—including of course the use of fossil fuels, the once and future boogeyman of climate change activism.

It was only in the 1990s that the principal concern about climate change activism shifted away from the risk of global cooling to a newfound concern about global *warming*. As global surface temperatures started to rebound, the climate change activists didn't celebrate progress or admit error. They simply redefined the threat while continuing to advocate for large-scale changes in human behavior, including foremost a reduction in the use of fossil fuels. Al Gore's famous documentary *An Inconvenient Truth* came out in 2006 and popularized this new concern about global warming.

Yet less than a decade after that film was released, a new inconvenient truth emerged for the climate activists: there was a three-year period from 2005 to 2008 during which global surface temperatures actually *declined* once again, just as they had generally in the pattern that raised the concerns about global cooling in the 1970s.[2]

Once again, the emergence of data points that ran contrary to apocalyptic predictions was a cause for neither celebration nor humility among those who warned of apocalypse. Instead they did the same thing they did in the 1990s: they changed their hypothesis again. That's when the entire supposed problem was reframed from "global warming" to "climate change."

This reframing was a particularly elegant sleight of hand because it shielded the central claim from falsifiability. In the 1990s, they took the cruder approach of simply *switching* the theory of catastrophe from global cooling to global warming—but if temperatures ever started to cool again, that would negate the new hypothesis. Inconveniently for the activists, that's exactly what started to happen.

But if you merely claim that the climate is "changing," you're effectively bulletproof from contradictory data. If temperatures go up, you get to claim victory. If temperatures go down, you get to claim victory. Even if temperatures stay *exactly flat*, but there is merely some undulation in other climate variables, you still get to claim victory.

VIVEK RAMASWAMY

This is the "no true Scotsman" fallacy on steroids. That's the logical fallacy named after the paradigmatic example coined by its inventor, Anthony Flew, who famously wrote: "No true Scotsman puts brown sugar on his porridge. The fact that Angus MacGregor puts brown sugar on his porridge just proves that he's no true Scotsman!"

No matter what happens to the climate, activists could claim victory to say it supported the existence of climate change—ignoring the fact that climate change has existed for as long as the earth has existed. The fact that their new hypothesis was unfalsifiable wasn't a bug; it's a *feature*. It's nothing short of remarkable that you didn't see *any* climate change activists or mainstream press comment on the three consecutive years of global surface temperature declines between 2005 and 2008. It is rank intellectual dishonesty.

But I want to be careful not to commit the same mistake: I *do* think the evidence tends to suggest that global surface temperatures appear to be gradually rising over the last half century—even though the magnitude is small and the trend is far from steady. Here's the hard data on it.

SO, IS THIS MAN-MADE?

If you read the lay press or most public distillations of the underlying science, you'd be convinced that human behavior is unambiguously responsible for the incremental rise in global surface temperatures.

The truth is a lot murkier.

One of the reasons why global surface temperatures appear to be going up may be an artifact of *measurement*. It turns out the ground tends to be hotter in areas where human beings have expanded their presence. The construction of roads with traffic lights, the use of motor vehicles, and the rise of buildings with indoor air-conditioning that expels heat outdoors all contribute to localized warming of the ground near areas of increased human activity.

GLOBAL AVERAGE SURFACE TEMPERATURE

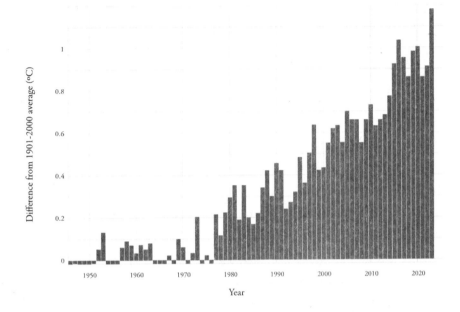

If you dig deep into the models of climate science, you'll find interesting fine print that includes these important caveats. In his book *Unsettled*, for instance, the climate scientist Steven Koonin breaks down a map of the east coast of the United States that ran in the *Washington Post* in August 2019, under the headline "Extreme Climate Change Has Arrived in America." At a first glance, the map appears to show exactly what the *Post* wants it to—large, deep red pockets that seem to suggest warming on a vast, irreversible scale.

Thanks to honest scientists such as Koonin, though, we can see that the truth is far more complicated.

"While the article might have you believe otherwise," he writes, "the *Post*'s maps do not illustrate the arrival of 'extreme climate change.' The localized blobs in these maps are not due to global climate changes, but instead are very likely the result of urbanization or the growth of human activities in rural areas that began producing oil and gas. In other words, the local climates of these areas may indeed have changed since the Industrial Revolution. Yet despite the article's frequent mention of greenhouse gases, these local changes have very little to do with global influences like these. For instance, carbon dioxide—the most important human-influenced greenhouse gas—exists in the atmosphere at roughly the same concentration all over the globe."[3]

Even if this is (or becomes) a truly global effect—from the cumulative sum total of increased urbanization around the world—this is not the *kind* of global surface temperatures that represents any cause for concern at all. The central claim of climate alarmists *isn't* that we should be worried if the ground is infinitesimally warmer at the end of this century than at the end of the last. Rather it's that rising surface temperatures are evidence of a broader change in the climate that could increase the frequency of extreme weather events that kill people, melt the polar ice caps that would increase sea levels that subsume helpless indigenous populations in the Pacific, and the rest of their parade of horribles. Yet if surface-temperature measurements on the ground are simply registering higher because of the expansion of human activity on the ground, that wouldn't be a cause for concern, even if you subscribe to the central claim of climate change activists.

The evidence for man-made global warming via changes to the atmosphere—rather than via the direct effect of increasing ground temperatures due to the expansion of human activity—is even more scant. Socially we have arrived at the consensus that CO_2 emissions are responsible for atmospheric changes. But these claims don't hold a scientific degree of certainty; on closer inspection, they look almost farcical. Take out a piece of paper and write down your guess of what percentage of the earth's atmosphere is composed of H_2O (water), CO_2 (carbon dioxide), N_2 (nitrogen), and other gases. Now compare them to the reality:

- Nitrogen (N_2): 78.08%
- Oxygen (O_2): 20.95%
- Argon (Ar): 0.93%

- Carbon dioxide (CO_2): 0.04%
- Water vapor (H_2O): from 0.2% to 4% depending on the location and weather conditions

The fact that CO_2 represents less than 0.1 percent of the gases in the earth's atmosphere, and that in absolute terms we see far greater variances of other gases like H_2O that are known to have their own greenhouse (heat-trapping) properties, makes it at least suspicious for the climate movement to have fixated its maniacal villain-finding focus on CO_2.

It becomes even more suspicious when you learn that the percentage of the atmosphere made up of CO_2 represents nearly an all-time low over the course of the history of the earth—yet the earth was more covered by glaciers for most of the period that CO_2 constituted a higher percentage of the atmosphere. Against that backdrop, an activist's concern that man-made emissions of CO_2 would have the effect of melting the polar ice caps should be suspicious. Add to that the fact that between 1979, when satellite measurements began being taken, and 2014, ice coverage in Antarctica *expanded*, and the narrative begins to fall apart.[4]

For the sake of argument, let's grant the most favorable version of the climate activist narrative for now: there is still evidence that global surface temperatures have tended to rise over the same period that human beings have increased their emissions of carbon dioxide, which is at least among the gases in the atmosphere known to contribute to a greenhouse effect. The claim of causality is more dubious than mainstream gatekeepers of information to the public will ever admit, but it turns out that's not even their biggest problem.

Even if we accept that global surface temperatures are rising, *and* that it's due to the man-made effect of increased CO_2 emissions, there is no reason to believe that this minuscule rise in global surface temperatures is actually a *net* negative for humanity.

And that's the third question to answer.

COULD A RISE IN TEMPERATURES BE A GOOD THING?

As strange as this question might look at first glance, there are basic reasons to believe that the answer might be yes. For instance, it's a fact that the earth is more covered by green surface area today than it was a century ago. Carbon dioxide is the most basic source of nourishment for plants and many plants tend to grow better in a slightly warmer climate. Even if you don't inherently accept that greater plant surface area coverage of the earth is inherently positive, plants are still the earth's natural and greatest carbon sink—suggesting that the earth has built-in equilibrating mechanisms to deal with incremental fluctuations in atmospheric gases like CO_2.

Against that backdrop, it's hardly a coincidence that environmental activists from the 1970s were more concerned about global deforestation and the supposed risks of reducing green surface area coverage when their cousins in the climate alarmist movement were warning about global *cooling*. Yet now that the climate narrative has shifted to an alarmist concern about global *warming*, the concerns about losing green surface area on earth have dissipated into the atmosphere.

Plant life on earth is hardly the greatest beneficiary of temperature increases. There's a much more direct benefit to human beings. Fewer humans will die on a planet where temperatures are incrementally warmer. Bjorn Lomborg, the head of Copenhagen Consensus and a visiting fellow at Stanford, has correctly observed that eight times as many people die of cold temperatures as warm ones. This is not just a contemporary phenomenon: in the course of human history, far more people have died from ice ages than heat waves. At the very least, this should make us question whether incrementally increased global surface temperatures is inherently a bad thing—or whether there are some positive effects that demand us to investigate further the costs and benefits.

Lomborg has also correctly noted that the most effective way to prevent all temperature-related deaths is to create more abundant access to fossil fuels—which of course runs contrary to the top prescription to fight global climate change.

On the topic of human death rates, there is another fact that's even more startling. In his seminal book *Fossil Future*, Alex Epstein notes that the climate-disaster-related death rate has declined by a staggering 98 percent over the course of the last century. Against the backdrop of media hysteria about the so-called climate emergency, it might be surprising to learn that a 98 percent reduction in climate-disaster-related deaths took place over precisely the same century that we saw the most dramatic increase in human use of fossil fuels. But there shouldn't be any surprise; the finding should be obvious: the reduction in deaths is *because* of more abundant access to, and usage of, fossil fuels to regulate temperatures, construct new buildings resistant to the effects of climate disasters, and so on.

So even if we grant that man-made behaviors are causally responsible for rising global temperatures (itself a dubious proposition), it's entirely possible that such changes in temperatures are a *positive* for humanity (as measured by death rates) and for earth (as measured by plant coverage of the surface). At minimum it requires far greater work to conclusively determine that a rise in temperatures will be *net* negative for humanity.

But suppose further that it *is* a net negative. The fourth and most pertinent question still remains: Are we certain that the alterations to human behavior required to reverse the effects of global warming will be more beneficial than harmful to humanity?

Or, phrased another way . . .

COULD THE CURE BE WORSE THAN THE DISEASE?

For years, we have been led to believe that fossil fuels are inherently evil. Even those of us who don't love the idea of insane activists defacing paintings and interrupting tennis matches tend to agree that we really *should* be using less oil and gas.

Again, the truth is much more complicated.

Over the past few decades, as the philosopher Alex Epstein has pointed out, "fossil fuels have powered the increased industrialization that has brought down the rate of extreme poverty—the percentage of people living on less than $2 a day—from *42 percent* in 1980 to less than 10 percent today."[5] Thanks to the widespread (and still increasing) use of fossil fuels, billions of people throughout the world have seen remarkable increases in the quality of their lives. Hospitals in these countries have been able to power respirators that keep people alive. They've been able to give life-saving care to babies who were born too early, and to detect problems in patients that would have been impossible to know about without access to the kind of reliable energy that fossil fuels provide.

In his book *Fossil Future*, Epstein recounts the story of a person who visited The Gambia, "one of many African countries that desperately lacks energy." In a diary entry, this person writes about being in a hospital on a Saturday afternoon. While there, she observes the lights flickering unexpectedly, which is unusual because "the lights never came on after 2 p.m. on the weekends." For the next few hours, the doctors scramble to take advantage of the sudden availability of energy. They deliver a baby via an emergency C-section, then deliver another who is premature, weighing only 3.5 pounds.

But the afternoon ends in tragedy. The baby who came out via C-section suffocates in the womb, and the doctors, who did not have enough power to use the ultrasound machine for each patient, were not able to detect the problems early enough. The premature baby dies shortly after it comes out of the womb. "Without reliable electricity," the visitor writes, "the hospital did not even contemplate owning an incubator."[6]

"Reliable electricity," she says, "is at the forefront of every staff member's thoughts. With it, they can conduct tests with electrically powered medical equipment, use vaccines and antibiotics requiring refrigeration, and plan surgeries to meet patients' needs. Without it, they will continue to give their patients the best care available, but in a country with an average life expectancy of only 54 years of age, it's a hard fight to win."[7]

Here in the United States, we have no idea what it's like to live this way. These were problems that we solved decades ago, when we used fossil fuels to bring electricity even to the most rural parts of the United States. Since then, we have relied on fossil fuels to power our electrical grids, our computers, and our streetlights. We have used this energy to become the most powerful nation in the world. It's no accident that the infant mortality rate in this country has decreased 90 percent since 1935, largely thanks to the energy provided by fossil fuels.

Now that other nations are attempting to do the same thing, climate change obsessives are telling them that the party is over. They're saying that it was perfectly fine for *us* to build up our country using cheap, reliable sources of energy. They're saying it was fine for China, India, and most of Europe as well. But now that African nations want to begin developing and make better lives for their people, it's time to stop.

If you'll notice, the anticolonialist, everything-is-racist crowd is nowhere to be found on this issue.

These people care only about what makes them look good in front of other activists. They don't care about poor people in developing countries, and they don't care about the millions of impoverished people in this country whose energy bills go up every time a new ridiculous scheme to reduce our fossil fuel consumption is enacted. Time and time again, I heard people on the campaign trail complain about the increasing costs of heating houses and filling cars with gas. Almost to a person, each said that it didn't seem like the people in our government cared about them or understood their problems.

One of them was a farmer in western Iowa whose family had been on her farm for generations. As we walked through her fields together, this farmer mentioned something that caught my attention. Her farm happened to be right in the path of a CO_2-capture pipeline that was ready to be constructed across the state. The government was going to tear up her land and build the pipeline whether she liked it or not.

It was the kind of thing she had probably shared with other politicians. Most of them, I assume, ignored her uncomfortable plea for help.

But I knew what it meant. It turns out that the CO_2 pipeline project in Iowa only existed because of federal subsidies that had been enacted by both major political parties, starting in the early 2000s under George W. Bush. The premise of these subsidies was to create incentives for private actors to capture CO_2 from manufacturing facilities—like ethanol production plants that are widespread in Iowa—and to be rewarded a certain amount of taxpayer cash per metric ton of CO_2 that they capture and sequester.

Getting the subsidies requires actually "sequestering" the CO_2—that is, *burying* the CO_2 in the ground. That's where the pipelines come in. First, they capture CO_2 emitted during the ethanol production process. Next, the CO_2 is pumped in pipelines across the states of Iowa, South Dakota, and North Dakota—where it is ultimately buried in the ground.

But here's the rub: many landowners and farmers don't want that CO_2 pipeline built in their backyard. And they're not just country bumpkins for thinking so. Some are concerned that the heavy equipment and construction will disrupt soil that hasn't been tilled for decades. Many are concerned about decreased crop yields—a very real possibility given the long-term destruction such pipelines have wreaked in the past.[8]

For a long time, I had been skeptical of carbon-capture technology, which seeks to take the CO_2 out of the air and bury it underground. I knew that the state could be extremely rough when it came to forcing farmers to consent to the construction of such pipelines.

I had also heard the story of what happened in Santaria, Mississippi, in February 2020.

SERIOUS DAMAGE

It was a little past seven o'clock in the evening when residents heard the blast.

Some saw the white mushroom cloud explode nearby. But no one knew what had happened. It got hard to breathe. Some people were unconscious. Cars stopped working. Combustion engines need oxygen, and the CO_2 layer had become so dense as it hovered near the ground that trucks and minivans were stranded on the highway. "It looked like you were going through the zombie apocalypse," Jack Willingham, the county emergency official who oversaw the rescue efforts, said.

A grandmother called 911 and was told that emergency vehicles couldn't get through either. No one was coming to rescue them. She put her two toddler grandchildren to bed, praying, not knowing if they would survive. Others were found slumped in their cars, unconscious, foaming at the nose and mouth, urine and excrement staining their clothes.

The mass poisoning lasted four hours, but its effects are still felt years later. Some are permanently disabled, including a former lumber mill worker who can no longer work due to muscle tremors and cognitive decline from the prolonged oxygen deprivation his brain suffered while unconscious during the leak. But all said, the rupture was not as bad as it easily could have been. "We got lucky," Willingham said. "If the wind blew the other way, if it'd been later when people were sleeping, we would have had deaths."

There is a sad irony to this tragedy: Climate zealots acknowledge that CO_2 is deadly, but to them, the solution is to concentrate, pressurize, and pump it through our communities under farms, homes, and schools—where it has maimed real, living people and will do so again in the future—rather than allowing it to escape safely into the atmosphere, where it may hypothetically, indirectly cause climate change that may (or may not) hurt some unknown person decades or centuries down the line.

This isn't right-wing propaganda: the pipelines are so dangerous that even climate-obsessed California has banned them in the state, finding the benefits to the planet, which are at best uncertain, aren't worth the risks. But given the money at stake, few people on the left or the right are willing to talk about these dangers.

Of course, at least when it comes to crop yields and soil fertility, land-owners are free to decide to take these risks if they want—but also to demand proper compensation for doing so. One farmer asked the pipeline company for shares in the project, since if he was taking individual risk, he wanted a small share of the uncapped profits that the project would generate. The answer was no. Others demanded more compensation than the proprietor desired to pay.

So they resorted to eminent domain—where the *government* compelled farmers to accept a fixed price to either sell their land or to provide an easement to the company that wanted to build the CO_2 pipeline across it, irrespective of whether the farmer agreed with the price or not.

That was the farmer's real grievance she shared as we walked the cow pasture. She didn't want a CO_2 pipeline built across her land. But there was a chance that it would happen *against her will*, her private property rights be damned.

I asked her exactly *why* it was so important to capture carbon dioxide and build a pipeline across farmland, over the objections of the owners of the land on whose property it was being constructed. I never got a clear answer to the question—other than the fact that "market forces" were demanding it, and that it was downstream of shifting global policy conditions in the fight against climate change.

Today, the acceptable range of public debate around CO_2 capture and sequestration concerns the extent to which the costs of a given project outweigh benefits that we take for granted. But the idea that there are any benefits in the first place often remains unquestioned. We're simply not allowed to ask that in polite society.

It's almost as though everyone involved in the debate in Iowa had forgotten the covers of *Time* and *Newsweek* magazines in the 1970s that had warned humanity against climate change of a very different kind—a global ice age that could threaten human existence. In a matter of fifty years, public concern had shifted to concern about the exact opposite result—an overheating of the planet—with elaborate policy prescriptions and steps to remove CO_2 from the atmosphere that would itself increase the very existential risk that climate scientists had warned of just a few decades earlier.

And who knows? We may return there once again. Fifty or a hundred years from now, we may once again fear global cooling. The next ice age. World leaders will be visiting elderly miners and engineers and drillers in nursing homes, scrambling to understand how they once dug up fossils and converted them into warmth. Countries will work frantically to fire up decaying coal plants, burning any and all carbon-based matter in a desperate attempt to raise the earth's temperature even a fraction of a degree.

It may sound far-fetched, but it's a thought experiment with a sounder scientific basis than the current climate orthodoxy.

Which, to be clear, isn't saying much.

WHO BENEFITS?

One group above all others stands to benefit from America's embrace of this new movement: the Chinese Communist Party (CCP). China benefits most from America's decline as an industrial power. Our increasingly complex and senseless climate agenda pressures manufacturers to send their factories abroad, where governments won't interfere with their ability to do business. Even when those companies move somewhere other than China, it's still a win for the CCP. Whenever production is taking place offshore, somewhere we may not be able to access in the event of war, that benefits China.

The greatest proponents of so-called "environmental, social, and governance" factors in U.S. capital markets are either inadvertently or expressly advancing Chinese interests at the expense of U.S. interests under the mantle of climate advocacy. BlackRock, the world's largest asset manager, often influences American businesses to take on a much higher standard of "corporate responsibility" than their Chinese counterparts. BlackRock, for example, in 2022 voted for "Scope 3 Emissions caps" at Chevron, one of the most important oil producers in America. Scope 3 emissions caps are the most aggressive form of constraints that an asset manager could apply to any company—because it requires a company to reduce not just its *own* emissions (Scope 1), but also those of certain business partners (Scope 2) and its entire supply chain (Scope 3). The business interest of Chevron in adopting Scope 3 emissions caps is the equivalent of McDonald's taking responsibility to reduce the weight of every customer who buys a Big Mac (as I argued in a shareholder letter that I wrote to Chevron in 2023 on behalf of Strive Asset Management).[9]

Yet it's puzzling that even though such emissions caps were adopted in the name of fighting global climate change, BlackRock also happened to be—*in that same year*—a large shareholder of PetroChina. Yet BlackRock's shareholder advocacy on global climate issues appears to have been limited to the West, not China. BlackRock never told PetroChina to adopt Scope 3 emissions caps or implement other "responsible" business practices. BlackRock seemed to be interested only in hamstringing an American company, not making global change.

The reason why the likes of BlackRock act this way is simple: it comes down to their own incentives. If BlackRock had tried to flex its muscle to the corporate board of PetroChina, the Chinese Communist Party would have told them to get the hell out of China. BlackRock enjoyed a special status as the only foreign firm with a full wholly owned subsidiary licensed to sell mutual funds to customers in mainland China.

By contrast, the U.S. government now creates incentives for the exact opposite. In 2022, the U.S. Department of Labor changed ERISA rules to expressly permit—and even encourage—asset managers like BlackRock to take into account nonpecuniary factors like climate change when allocating capital and behaving as a shareholder. The Securities and Exchange Commission (SEC), the most important regulator governing the asset management industry, has tried for the last two years to implement mandatory climate risk disclosures to investors—of the exact kind that would validate the likes of Larry Fink, CEO of BlackRock. So if Black-Rock adopts climate constraints through its capital allocation and proxy voting behaviors as a shareholder of U.S. companies, but not of Chinese ones, BlackRock is doing exactly what is in its *own* best financial interests both in the U.S. and in China.

It's a parallel example to why the sponsor of the CO_2 pipeline in Iowa—an elaborate project pipeline predicated on the importance of removing CO_2 from the atmosphere—is also one of the largest ethanol producers in Brazil.

It makes sense for financially motivated actors to act according to their financial incentives. This should surprise no one. What makes less sense is why ordinary—and mostly earnest—climate change activists are going along with it, even though it makes very little sense even to advance their own self-stated objectives, without critically analyzing why.

It goes back to the hard truth that God is real. When you fail to recognize that ultimate truth, you start making up substitutes for it instead. Nearly every culture in human history has sought to change the climate. Shamans in ancient China danced with rings of fire until their drops of sweat created rain. Scandinavian witches are said to have claimed the power to control the wind, selling it to sailors who feared the misfortune of calm winds stranding their ships at sea. Indonesians placed rice and fruit in makeshift boats and floated them down a river to prevent volcanic eruption.[10] The Toltecs and Aztecs sacrificed children to bring good weather, often torturing them beforehand to ensure their tears would satisfy the gods.[11] Our innate hubris tells us that we can change the universe around us through our own agency, a psychological tendency that extends much further back than the present moment.

FIVE TRUTHS

1. In the 1970s, climate alarmists warned that "global cooling" would end humanity. Just thirty years later, the same climate alarmists warned that global *warming* would end humanity. Both are false.
2. Measurements of global warming are far more complicated than scientists have been willing to admit—as detailed by physicist Steven Koonin, who served in the U.S. Department of Energy under President Barack Obama, in his book *Unsettled.*
3. Contrary to popular narratives, warmer temperatures have positive effects on humanity. Eight times as many people die of cold temperatures each year as warm ones, and the best way to prevent all temperature-related deaths is by doing the exact opposite of what climate alarmists call for: providing greater access to reliable energy.
4. More people have died due to the global policy response to climate change than have died of climate change itself.
5. Climate change policies hurt the West and benefit China, which fails to adopt climate-related constraints and instead produces batteries and other inputs for the new "green economy"—which directly increases U.S. dependence on China.

3

"AN OPEN BORDER IS NOT A BORDER"

Here's a fundamental truth: Borders define a nation. They are, quite literally, what defines its territory, its citizenry, and its sovereign reach from that of a neighboring land. A nation without borders is not a nation. This is almost tautologically true.

Here's a second truth: There are more people who would like to come to the United States than the current citizens of the United States are willing and able to take in.

According to analysis conducted by the Center for Immigration Studies, some 700 million people worldwide would like to migrate to the United States, given the opportunity. Accepting them all would triple the number of U.S. residents overnight.[1] For every U.S. citizen, there would be two brand-new immigrants, mostly from Africa and Central and South America. That's simply not tenable.

Those figures are based on a simple Gallup poll, true, and it's easy enough to tell the phone surveyor you'd be willing to come when asked. But our green-card lottery system reveals a similar truth. In 2023, almost 10 million people applied for just 55,000 spots. Residents from some countries found the U.S. more alluring than others. In 2020, nearly 12 percent of the population of Sierra Leone applied for a green card to come to the United States, around 950,000 applications in a country of just 8 million people.[2] That's a lot of interest. But consider that under our green-card lottery system, the chosen few are allowed to bring their family. That means each household only needs to apply once. Sierra Leone's average household size is six people.[3]

Taken together, the numbers reflect that nearly every man, woman, and child in Sierra Leone not only desires to migrate to the United States, but has taken affirmative steps to make it happen. Virtually everyone. It's a level of popularity that makes Taylor Swift look like Nancy Pelosi.

America has built something special, something that is the envy of the world. Sometimes we take for granted how good we have it. People from other countries don't. But unless we're willing to radically throw open the doors to all comers—something literally no one supports— we simply cannot accept everyone.

That means one thing: We must choose.

HOW DO WE DECIDE?

There are many possibilities. One is to select people based on luck. This is something like the green-card lottery, technically known as the "Diversity Visa Program," that we have now. There are pluses. It seems fair. Everyone has a roughly equal shot. And who wouldn't want a nation filled with lucky winners? But we can probably do better.

Another possibility is that, maybe, we want to select people based on hardship. There is some merit to this contention. From a strictly utilitarian standpoint, opening the doors of American prosperity to people who are the worst-off would do the most good. It also runs in the spirit of Lady Liberty's promise to bring her the world's tired, poor, huddled masses and all that.

There's a flavor of this principle that runs through our current immigration system. One is the humanitarian-based temporary protection status the president can give to migrants from nations struck by turmoil. As the name implies, it's supposed to be temporary, but (shockingly) it's usually not. Haitians who came to the U.S. after the 2010 earthquake, for instance, still haven't gone home. When President Donald Trump decided not to renew their "temporary" status in 2018, Haitians sued, claiming he was terminating the program based on racial animus. They lost the case, but not before President Joe Biden took office and renewed their status once again. But however flawed, humanitarian resettlement programs represent just a fraction of overall immigration.

The much larger version of this selecting-for-hardship policy is the refuge we provide to the massive number of people showing up at our border. Nearly all of them are economic migrants hoping to come to America for a better life. But at least on paper, that's not what our asylum system is for. Our system is for *refugees*. And that has a very specific meaning in the law.

To be eligible for asylum, an alien must prove that they are fleeing persecution. That means that if they're forced to return home, they have a well-founded fear that they would be persecuted—that is, suffer bodily harm or death—on account of race, religion, nationality, political opinion, or membership in a particular social group. What does that mean? Well, it means that if you're a Tutsi raped by a Hutu because of your ethnicity, you're allowed in; if you're a woman raped by a drunk soldier because she looks like easy prey, that doesn't count.[4] If you're hunted down and beaten because you're Christian in a Muslim nation, you can get asylum; if you're beaten because you refuse to join a Mexican cartel or pay them protection money, you cannot. Needless to say, simply being poor and enduring substandard living conditions doesn't get close to clearing the bar.

If these standards sound extreme, it's because they are. The regime rose from the ashes of World War II. It was meant to prevent a situation where Jews needed somewhere to go to flee Nazi Germany, and were met with armed forces sending them back. It's meant to prevent another voyage of the *St. Louis*, when in 1939 America turned away 937 Jewish refugees who had finally reached Florida's shores; after their return to Europe, 254 died during the war, most at concentration camps.[5] We can't have that happen again. But America's compassion is not an invitation for abuse. An asylum seeker's situation must be dire.

That's why the rules also require that there be no possibility of resettlement within the country you are fleeing from. If a Tijuana, Mexico, woman would be able to flee domestic violence by moving to León, or a Guatemalan teen who refuses to join an urban gang could escape to a remote mountain town and make a life as a goat farmer, that's their recourse. They may not like it, but if they'd like to come to the U.S. for a more prosperous life, they can enter the green-card lottery like everyone else. Our asylum laws are meant to provide a safe haven for refugees only in the most extreme cases of countrywide political persecution, where the persecuted have literally nowhere else to go. When coming to America is a matter of life or death.

That's not the situation facing most migrants today.

CHEATING THE SYSTEM

Many of the current migrants aren't even the most *economically* deprived. They come to the United States to climb the next rung of the ladder, not to stave off starvation.

Casas de remesas, or "remittance houses," are a big draw.[6] They're large, American-style mansions that have popped up all over Guatemala and Mexico, an emblem of the riches and success one can earn if he ventures north. "A lot of people started to see a lot of people going to the U.S. starting to build big houses, and we wanted the same," Guatemalan Francisco Santizo explained.[7] They work in the U.S. for a few growing seasons, then retire in luxury in Central America. In one town, all but 300 of the 1,500 residents have left. There are no gangs. No violence. "Crime is so absent we don't even need a police officer," one resident explained. These people aren't fleeing persecution. They aren't even fleeing poverty. And given their intent to return, they aren't even really fleeing.

Not that it matters. In America, so long as you utter the word *asylum* at the border, you'll be shown through the door, with years of freedom in the United States as your case winds its way through the immigration system. That's more than enough to spring for the wraparound porch and six-bedroom suite. And that's assuming you decide to show up for court at all.

The news is flooded with stories of caravans overflowing with desperately impoverished women and children, making a dangerous trek over land for thousands of miles. *Who would undertake such a treacherous journey*, one might think, *unless they had no other choice?* Forget the fact that the vast majority of illegal aliens are single adults, mostly working-age males.[8]

And in any event, arriving by caravan is quickly becoming passé. There's a new way many so-called refugees are coming to America, although they rarely admit it once they've crossed: by a prepaid vacation, complete with flights, hotels, and perhaps a few days at the beach. Facebook and Instagram are full of ads for "tourist agencies" offering chartered trips.[9] The agencies even throw in a tour guide to help with the final few steps of the journey, advising vacationers to toss their passports and concoct a more harrowing tale. But at $8,000 to $10,000 per ticket, do you really think Colombia's or West Africa's most crushingly impoverished people are taking these tours?

More entrepreneurial travelers, of course, can book flights on their own. One Colombian raved about the experience, spending two nights at a resort in Cancún before flying to an airport closer to the border and hopping over by foot, surrendering herself to border officials in broad daylight.[10] Another Venezuelan woman flew into Mexicali and took a cab to the border, crossed, and was soon on her way to the airport to catch another flight to Delaware. She could have tried to cross by land, but why would she? "This was so much easier," she explained.[11] Of course it was.

But if and when they show up for their asylum hearing, the story often changes. It becomes a contest of who can tell the tallest, most harrowing tale while keeping the details straight.

The *New York Times* profiled one woman, a Russian migrant who sought asylum in Brooklyn.[12] A lesbian, who fled Putin's oppressive, hateful regime. A place where no member of the LGBTQ+ community could ever feel safe. Her attorney began pressing her on her romantic history, to make sure she'd have all the details down when asked by the immigration judge. Finally, the woman broke down. "I'm not gay at all," she said. "I don't even like gay people."[13]

This is what our system has become: a victim Olympics where the victors are not even those who have suffered the most, but the ones most willing to cheat.

But in truth, our current immigration system isn't even doing *that*. The single most important factor in determining whether an applicant will be granted asylum isn't how much they've suffered or how good a tale they can tell.

It's something else entirely: what judge they happen to be assigned.

In San Francisco, there is one immigration judge who grants 98.5 percent of all asylum claims she hears.[14] But another judge, on the same court, grants just 4.6 percent.[15] The petitions, it should be noted, are distributed at random. San Francisco is not alone. In Houston, there is a judge who has denied every single asylum petition he's considered in the past five years; not a single applicant has been able to get through. His New York colleagues, however, are much more generous, with a dozen judges granting asylum claims at a rate of 80 percent or more.

It's mayhem. Such dramatically different success rates reflect a grave disrespect for the rule of law. People sometimes complain that the Supreme Court is a partisan tribunal divided along party lines, but the truth is that a 9–0 outcome is much more common than 5–4. The law is the law. Most of the time, everyone agrees. And critically, the Supreme Court *picks* which cases it is going to hear. Naturally, it picks the close cases, the ones where there's confusion in the courts below, where judges are most prone to disagree. In the lower appellate courts, judges from all political stripes reach unanimous outcomes nearly all the time. It doesn't really matter which panel of judges you get. Most cases are easy to decide. Everyone tends to agree. But immigration court is different. *Very* different.

The conclusion is inescapable: When it comes to our immigration system, no one is following the law. *Not even the judges themselves.*

HOW DO WE FIX IT?

Step one is obvious: seal the border. Writing new laws doesn't matter if we don't mean what we say. That means more enforcement, fewer admissions, more deportations. No more catch-and-release. You are encouraged to apply for asylum from outside the United States. If you show up at our border unannounced, you will be detained. If you do not meet the criteria for asylum, you will be expelled.

That's how Australia does it. Nearly everyone who arrives uninvited is detained until their asylum claim is heard. And you know what? It works. People don't bother trying to come if they know they won't get in. As a result, just 20 percent of Australia's asylum applicants are found to be fraudulent.

Would this require more border resources? More detention facilities? More physical barriers? More border patrolmen? In the short term, absolutely. But in the long term, we'd spend a lot less. If we invest in border security now, fewer people will come.

There are other ways to change incentives too. We could look closely at a "safe third country" policy. The idea is that refugees are entitled to refuge *somewhere*, but not necessarily in their country of choice. The Jews fleeing Nazi Germany weren't exactly picky, after all. For that reason, our immigration laws allow the president to designate other countries that asylum seekers must apply to first. Right now, only Canada is on our list, meaning that asylum seekers who try to enter via our northern border must explain why they didn't apply for asylum in Canada first. But there is zero reason why that should be the case. Migrants who have been able to escape their home countries should be required to apply for asylum in the first foreign country they set foot in, regardless of whether the migrant would prefer to live somewhere else.

The idea isn't outlandish. Look at Britain. They've gone even further, enacting a new policy where asylum seekers will wait in Rwanda for their claims to be heard. The economics alone are compelling. The UK estimates it will spend $12,000 on a one-way ticket for each refugee (which, frankly, seems high; Expedia has flights from Heathrow to Kigali for around $300) and pay another $25,000 to Rwanda for taking them in, providing room and board, etc. That's $37,000 in all. Of course, it's worth noting that at this point, the United Kingdom has moved almost no one to Rwanda, so this scheme may never work.

Compare that to what we're spending now. U.S. Immigration and Customs Enforcement (ICE) estimates that it costs about $150 per day to detain border jumpers; grassroot organizations estimate it's more like $200. So let's call it $175.

Now we need to figure out how long someone is typically detained. ICE's official documents say the average wait time was 55 days in 2019. But that number is skewed, because a ton of people who are caught and detained immediately give up and go back home. (Which alone is pretty telling.) The people who stick it out are detained longer. How much longer is not totally clear, but a 2013 lawsuit revealed that the typical California ICE detainee seeking relief from removal was detained for 421 days.[16]

Using these figures—and it's a back-of-the-envelope calculation, to be sure—the U.S. spends an average of about $74,000 per alien it detains.

Thirty-seven thousand dollars for a trip to Rwanda, by comparison, is a downright bargain.

Why on earth should taxpayers be spending an additional $40,000 per alien to detain them in a cell with four walls that happens to be located in Texas, rather than Rwanda or Mexico or somewhere else? Surely we can think of *some* better way for taxpayer money to be spent.

But it gets better. Under the UK plan, migrants whose claims are denied are sent back home. Nothing new there. But migrants whose claims are successful are offered safe residency—*in Rwanda*. In other words, win, lose, or draw, uninvited migrants who show up on the UK's shores *will not be staying* in the UK.

"If people know there is no place for them there, they won't come," lamented one Afghan migrant in Britain.[17] That's the point.

Human rights critics are trying to shut down the program, claiming Rwanda isn't safe. That's just their bigotry talking. In truth, Rwanda has about half the homicide rate of the United States, and about one-tenth the murder rate of Chicago. Releasing migrants into Yuma, Arizona, or busing them to the Windy City is far more dangerous.

We also need to end birthright citizenship. It's an invitation for abuse. Or an opportunity for aspiring entrepreneurs, depending on how you look at it. For $30,000 to $100,000, wealthy women from China, Russia, Nigeria, and elsewhere can fly to the U.S., stay in private Beverly Hills mansions and boutique Miami homes, give birth in the U.S., and return home, knowing that their child now has American citizenry.[18] It's like a "stay in a good hotel," one mother explained.[19] It's a kind of insurance policy too. Their children now have the option to live here any time they like; in time, they'll be able to bring over their parents too.

Many people, including today's State Department, seem to think there's little we can do to combat birth tourism. The Constitution automatically confers citizenship on anyone born here, they believe. But the Constitution actually says no such thing. Instead, the Fourteenth Amendment says that citizenship extends to "[a]ll persons born or naturalized in the United States, *and subject to the jurisdiction thereof.*"

It's a peculiar phrase. But its presence is no accident. According to the principal authors of the clause, Senators Lyman Trumball of Illinois and Jacob Howard of Ohio, the phrase means "[n]ot owing allegiance to anybody else." That's what the Supreme Court has said too. In the 1873 *Slaughter-House Cases*, the Supreme Court said the phrase was intended "exclude from [birthright citizenship] children of ministers, consuls, and citizens or subjects of foreign States, born within the United States." And in the 1884 case *Elks v. Wilkin*, the Court found that children born to members of Indian tribes did not have birthright citizenship because these children were subject to tribal jurisdiction, not that of the United States. It wasn't until the Indian Citizenship Act of 1924 that Native Americans obtained citizenship through birth. Under our Constitution, even birthright citizenship is only available to those who have submitted to our jurisdiction, and that includes playing by the rules that citizenship requires.

"Seal the border" means more than just build a wall in the literal sense. It's about incentives. And consequences. Once we put up a "we're closed" sign on the door—and enforce it—people will get the message.

But when one door closes, another one opens. That's step two: making conscious decisions about *legal* immigration. Who we actually want to admit. That means thinking critically about who we want to be our future friends and neighbors, and why.

One possibility is to select based on merit. To welcome the best and the brightest. Canada has embraced such a policy, where most green cards are given based on a 100-point scale, with points awarded to applicants having higher education or specialized expertise. Other countries have too. Following Canada's early lead, in the 2000s, Australia, Denmark, Japan, and the UK all adopted a version of it.[20]

The great thing about a points system is that you don't have to select purely based on "merit" in the smartest, most talented, most educated, hardest-working, most-"deserving" applicant sense (although you can certainly use it to select for that too). A points-based system can also select for other traits, like hard work and willingness to contribute where America needs it most. That means taking a careful look at our country's economic and labor market needs. In Australia, PhDs get extra points, yes, but so do people with experience in in-demand fields, like car mechanics. In the U.S. we could award points for people willing to work as home health care aides or seasonal farmworkers. And we could adjust as our labor market changes, as more or fewer American workers are willing and able to fill certain jobs.

Another possibility: we could select for the ability to acclimate. This means things like speaking English or demonstrating an understanding and respect for our shared American history and culture, including passing a civics test. It could also mean favoring or disfavoring applicants from countries that either embrace or are openly hostile to American values like treating women as equal citizens, allowing freedom of expression, and embracing other Western ideals.

A further consideration: we could use immigration as a foreign policy tool. To share our values, to spread the virtues of capitalism and democracy, our love of freedom, to the rest of the world. Our student exchange programs recognize this. So does our au pair program, which allows a foreigner to live with a host family for up to two years to provide low-cost childcare before returning home.

Living in America is a privilege. It is the ultimate carrot. There are many countries that would like their students to train here, to do cutting-edge research, to learn from the top doctors, scientists, and engineers in the world, and to bring that knowledge back home. But a privilege is not a right. If China refuses to stem the tide of Chinese-manufactured fentanyl washing onto our shores, killing countless young Americans, then our doors should be closed to young Chinese seeking student visas to study here. If the Colombian government wants to make millions guiding South American migrants north to our doorstep, then it should be cut off from free trade with the United States.[21] If Venezuela won't take its criminals back, then its business executives should no longer be able to vacation in Aspen or buy up homes in Miami.[22]

It's not that complicated. Just as individuals should not be free to disrespect our immigration laws when they find it convenient, governments should not be able to do so either. That's America First.

Progressives may object to this way of thinking as considering only American interests, as opposed to those of migrants or the world at large. They may even argue that such a framework commodifies migrants, dehumanizes them, and ignores their plight.

To this I offer a few responses. First, the obligations of a nation run not only primarily, but exclusively, to its citizens. That is what makes a nation a nation. It is what differentiates a nation from an empire or an authoritarian regime bent on world domination. Our leadership is the government of the United States, not the United Nations, and not the World Goodness Committee.

Further, claims that an organized, disciplined, numerically capped legal immigration system would hurt our standing on the world stage are not only irrelevant, but overblown. Japan and South Korea allow almost no immigration; when unemployment rises, Japan has even paid migrants to go back home. These practices may catch flak in the back pages of the *New York Times*, but no one else seems to notice, much less care. Turkey, for its part, has drawn praise for holding tens of thousands of Syrian refugees in container camps with medical care, grocery stores, and even barbershops, but the thought of allowing these refugees free entry into its country, to integrate permanently with its citizenry, is off the table.[23] Yet America is somehow expected to hand every migrant a Social Security card and warm hand towel at the border.

The double standard would be appalling, but, in truth, there's not really any standard at all. Different countries, and different people within those countries, have very different views of whether a nation has a legal or ethical obligation to accept migrants, and on what terms. There is no one-size-fits-all solution. And in any event, we're not in middle school. We shouldn't be making policy decisions based on how popular they will make us in the eyes of other people.

But even if the United States had a moral obligation to improve the plight of every man, woman, and child on earth, regardless of citizenship, residency, or connection to America, throwing open our borders would not be the way to do it. It's like universal basic income. It may sound compassionate on paper, helping the neediest by giving a certain amount of cash to everyone, but once everyone has an additional $500 a month, no one does. Inflation spirals. The price of rent and groceries goes up by more than the $500 check. A dollar is worth less. Everyone is worse off. The same would be true if we became a borderless nation.

But what about the children? Surely they deserve a safe place to live, to grow, to go to school? And surely we, as Americans, can find the generosity within us to share the prosperity of our great nation with the youngest, most innocent, most vulnerable foreigners?

I agree there is certainly room in our immigration policies for citizens to open their homes to alleviate the suffering of children abroad. One way is to continue to allow loving American families to adopt foreign orphans—although we must be ever vigilant to avoid creating incentives for baby mills or human trafficking or worse.[24] Another is to encourage private charity to help children in developing nations. People forget sometimes that Americans are the most generous people in the world. We outgive every other country on the planet, not just in raw numbers, but as a percentage of gross domestic product (GDP), by a margin of more than two to one.

But the way our current border policies try to "help" children causes nothing but harm. Children are now the "get out of jail free" card for border crossers, ensuring they will not be detained. And the coyotes, the smugglers, know it. That's because in 2015 a progressive California judge held that children could not be detained for more than twenty days.[25]

Logically, that leaves one of two options: either the parents are released with the child, or the parents are detained while the child is released.

President Trump, of course, opted for door two, the much-decried "child separation" policy. But riddle me this: If an American citizen is caught committing a crime with her toddler in tow, what happens? Does the arresting officer say, "I'm so sorry, miss. I didn't realize you had a baby. Naturally, I cannot separate a mother from her child, so you are free to go"? Not in a million years. She is arrested. And her baby will be placed with a family member or in foster care until her case is resolved and she has served her time. Over 150,000 mothers are imprisoned in the United States. None of their children are imprisoned along with them. Yet when ICE follows the exact same protocol for an illegal alien caught crossing our border, the left decries it as a human rights abuse.

Hypocrisy aside, the policy has done nothing but turn children into human shields. From 2015 to 2021, there was a tenfold increase in adults crossing with minor children. This is not a coincidence. Mothers are renting out their children to accompany single men over the border.[26] Border patrol has fought to keep up.[27] In 2019, they began using rapid DNA tests to see if these children were truly related. In somewhere between 8.5 percent and 30 percent of cases, there was no genetic relation at all.[28]

The left's response? Blood does not make a family. There are other kinds of families—stepfamilies, adoptive families, chosen families, polyamorous families—that are equally valid. DNA tests are tools that the privileged class uses to elevate one heteronormative type of family over others.

In other words, when confronted with irrefutable evidence of child trafficking, the left's response is to decry "cultural insensitivity."

They must have forgotten common sense at the door. Canada knows better than to even *risk* that a parent is absconding with a child without the consent of both legal parents. But under the left's preferred policy, if a twenty-year-old single migrant male comes to Eagle Pass, Texas, with a child strapped to his back, claims the child is his, and then DNA refutes that claim, we're supposed to usher the "father-son" duo across an international border, ideally with an apology for having forced him to take the test.

Mercifully, the Biden administration has recently decided to stop this charade: by pulling the plug on the testing. That's right. Just like when the SAT reveals that Asian Americans tend to score higher in math, the solution isn't to address the underlying issue, but to stop using the test. Blame the messenger, in twenty-three pairs of chromosomes or less.

Still, I empathize with the people who want to come here, children and adults alike. In my role as a presidential candidate, my highest and sole purpose was to help American citizens. The people of our country.

But as a private citizen—as a human—I understand the deep-seated desire to strive for a better life and the willingness to take great risks to do so.

Immigration is a deeply personal issue for me. I'm a child of immigrants. *Legal* immigrants. That's not just a talking point, not just a bullet on my Wikipedia page. It's my life. This country has given so much to my parents. To me. But that's precisely why it's so important to get it right. To be thoughtful. To create a system that is fair. That is transparent. That is honest. That reflects America's values. So that the next generation of Americans—those born here and those who are not—can fully participate in democratic life and continue to build on the promise of our nation.

FIVE TRUTHS
1. Borders define a nation's territory, citizenry, and sovereignty; without them, a nation simply cannot exist.
2. With 700 million people worldwide wanting to migrate to the U.S., it's clear we can't take everyone without overwhelming our resources and infrastructure.
3. The U.S. asylum system is specifically for those fleeing persecution due to race, religion, nationality, political opinion, or social group membership, not for those seeking economic opportunities or escaping general hardships.
4. Asylum approval rates vary wildly depending on the judge, from nearly 100 percent to as low as 4.6 percent, which shows a

concerning lack of consistency and respect for the rule of law in immigration courts.

5. Stronger border control and reformed asylum policies, like those in Australia, which detain nearly all uninvited asylum seekers, significantly reduce fraudulent claims and manage migrant flows more effectively.

4

THERE ARE TWO GENDERS

In ordinary times, the more obvious a statement is, the less likely it is to be controversial. But we don't live in ordinary times. Today there is often an *inverse* relationship between the obviousness of a statement and how controversial it is.

And there is no statement more obvious, while generating more mass controversy, than this one: there are *two* genders.

When I faced off with Chuck Todd as a presidential candidate during one of his final interviews as the host of NBC's *Meet the Press*, he challenged me on how I could be so certain of that proposition when "scientists" now believed otherwise. I didn't invoke my summa cum laude Harvard biology degree, because that would have made me the most insufferable character on the NBC network, and I wouldn't want to take that mantle from Joy Reid. The fact that I'd passed my sixth-grade science class at public school in southwest Ohio would have sufficed. If you have two X chromosomes, you're a woman. If you have an X and a Y chromosome, you're a man. That's stone-cold, hard biological reality.

Indeed for nearly all of recorded medical history, that was accepted as incontrovertible truth. In psychiatry, the definition of a "delusion" is a fixed, false belief. That's when a person believes something for an extended period that plainly contradicts objective truth. Physicians use a diverse array of therapies to treat people who suffer from delusions—from patients who believe they are cats to those who believe that their loving family members are carrying out an elaborate plot to kill them. That's why those who suffer from gender dysphoria—the fixed, false belief that your gender does not match your biological sex—have long been viewed to suffer from a mental health disorder. Physicians across the Western world agreed on this all the way through the publication of the *Diagnostic and Statistical Manual of Mental Disorders, Fifth Edition* (*DSM-5*), the world's most authoritative catalog of mental disorders. That's a hard fact in the history of medicine.

Yet if you say any of those things out loud in our modern era, you risk losing your job, public castigation by elites, or being censored on the internet.

That's not hyperbole.

Consider the case of J. K. Rowling. As recently as five years ago, Rowling was beloved by people from all over the political spectrum for the magical world she created in the Harry Potter book series, stories that were of course adapted into major films. Today she's been blacklisted by Hollywood and condemned even by the actors who were made famous by her characters—all because she dared to point out (quite mildly, in my opinion) that there is such a thing as biological sex.

In 2019 she defended Maya Forstater, a woman in the United Kingdom who was brought before a tribunal at work (and ultimately fired) because she criticized the UK government for allowing people to self-identify their gender.[1]

"Dress however you please," she wrote in the eminently reasonable tweet. "Call yourself whatever you like. Sleep with any consenting adult who'll have you. Live your best life in peace and security. But force women out of their jobs for stating that sex is real? #IStandWithMaya #ThisIsNotADrill."[2]

The reaction was swift. Activists called it hate speech. Death threats rolled in. But Rowling—who has enough money to be more than secure for the rest of her life—didn't back down. In the years since, she's called out dangerous policies such as youth transition, so-called "bathroom bills," and a recent law in Scotland that makes misgendering someone a literal crime. For that she's faced a nonstop torrent of threats to her life and safety for years. As Rowling told host Megan Phelps-Roper during a podcast about her life in 2023, she has received so many death threats that she could "paper [her] house with them," including one that said, "I wish you nice pipe bomb in mailbox."[3] Protests have been staged outside her house, and her address has been posted online.

Fortunately, J. K. Rowling has the means to hire private security. Most people don't. In the United States, the journalist Jesse Singal was met with a similar campaign of harassment after he published a balanced, well-researched story in the *Atlantic* titled "When Children Say They're Trans." The article, which went viral for its willingness to point out that many children who undergo gender transition therapy later regret the decision, caused an uproar among activists. Many sent death threats. A campaign to falsely paint Singal as some kind of sexual harasser with an ax to grind against trans women almost succeeded.[4] Today he hosts a podcast with Katie Herzog—another journalist who was blackballed after publishing a piece critical of trans activism—and still does excellent work.

But not everyone has been so fortunate. Every day, ordinary citizens are shadow-banned and throttled on social media for daring to go against the trans ideology. In 2019, a Canadian blogger named Meghan Murphy was banned from Twitter for using male pronouns to refer to a trans woman named Jessica Yaniv. She also referred to Yaniv, who was in the news because Yaniv had filed a complaint against a salon that had refused to perform a Brazilian wax on Yaniv, by Yaniv's former name, thereby engaging in a practice known as "deadnaming." This is just a case that made the news; thousands more occur every day.

As the writer Chaya Rachik has pointed out, this forces people to lie. It categorizes using "the correct sex based pronouns for someone" as "harassment." But for LGBTQIA+ advocacy groups, it doesn't go far enough. They'd rather see anyone who violates the policy banned forever. "This," wrote a spokesman for the advocacy group GLAAD, "effectively means that enormous quantities of dangerous anti-trans hate and harassment will remain active on the platform—causing harm to trans and nonbinary people who see it."[5]

Nearly every major institution—from universities to social media platforms to Fortune 500 companies—has responded to the pressure in the same way. With very few exceptions, they've swallowed the trans narrative whole, refusing out of fear to question the insane arguments of this movement.

For the rest of this chapter, I'll examine several of the trans movement's "arguments" in detail. We'll begin with the most common and most easily disprovable one—which isn't so much an argument as it is a refrain.

"THE SCIENCE IS SETTLED"

In February 2023, shortly after the *New York Times* published a surprisingly honest, balanced account of the evidence for so-called "gender-affirming care" in children, a black truck appeared outside the headquarters of the newspaper in Manhattan. On its giant LED screen, amid a sea of overheated rhetoric, these words appeared in red type.

The science is settled.[6]

Now, let's leave aside for a moment that the science surrounding socalled gender-affirming care is anything but settled. Recently a five-year investigation into youth gender medicine in the United Kingdom revealed serious cracks in the foundations of gender medicine. The findings of this study were conducted by a nonpartisan doctor named Hilary Cass. Among other things, the Cass Report found that while "a considerable amount of research had been published in [the] field, systematic evidence reviews demonstrated the poor quality of the published studies, meaning there is not a reliable evidence base upon which to make clinical decisions."[7]

What's more interesting is that the "follow-the-science" crowd finds the invocation of objective science to be offensive depending on the political context. Here that political context is the increasing popularity—and power—wielded by self-labeled LGBTQIA+ crusaders across American culture. Yet the fact that lesbians, gays, bisexuals, transgenders, queers, intersex, and asexual individuals are amalgamated into a single category itself raises certain logical fallacies that contradict science too.

Consider the following. A core tenet of the gay and lesbian segments of this movement is that the sex of the person you're *attracted* to is hardwired on the day you're born. That was actually the foundational premise of the gay rights movement.

It had to be. If homosexuality didn't count as an "immutable characteristic" in the eyes of the law, there would be no basis for treating discrimination on the basis of sexual orientation in the same way we treat discrimination on the basis of race or gender. The underlying intuition is that it's fair game for employers or others in civil society to draw distinctions between different individuals based on the *choices* they make, yet it's unfair and inhumane to discriminate against someone for characteristics they inherited on the day they were born and have no power to change. By successfully arguing that being gay is immutably set on the day you're born, the LGBTQIA+ political movement took off the table historical attempts at "conversion therapy" or denying service or employment based on sexual orientation.

I'm not contesting the premise that being gay is inherited at birth, but it's worth noting that the scientific backing for that proposition is shockingly scarce. For example, there's no such thing as a "gay gene" that's been identified. No credible scientist believes that one ever will be either. In fact there isn't even strong evidence of a genetic fingerprint or epigenetic hallmark of any kind for homosexuality. The absence of any biological basis—genetic, epigenetic, or otherwise—at least raises certain hard questions about whether homosexuality is *truly* an immutable characteristic hardwired at birth.

The ship has long sailed on the acceptance of gay marriage in America, and to be clear I'm not arguing against marriage equality, as some clown in the mainstream media will surely claim based on my willingness to even ask this question. In fact I'm *opposed* to political attempts to unwind gay marriage in the U.S.—it's a legally settled matter that would do more harm than good to our nation to relitigate.

I raise the question for a different reason. It's considered beyond the pale today to raise the idea that homosexuality might not be an immutable characteristic, despite the near-total absence of any biological basis to make that claim. Yet the exact same LGBTQIA+ movement that steadfastly says the sex of the person you're attracted to *must* be hardwired on the day you're born—and that anyone who questions that premise is a de facto bigot—is also the same movement that now says that your own sex is an entirely *mutable* characteristic over the course of your life.

This is especially strange, because there *is* an incontrovertible genetic basis for your biological sex. It's not a single gene, it's an entire chromosome—visible to even an untrained eye on basic genetic karyotyping. There are clear anatomical organs visible to the naked eye that are definitively associated with those chromosomes—and have been for the entirety of human history. Women have two X chromosomes; a uterus and vagina; they are able to give birth to children. Men have an X and Y chromosome; a penis and testicles; they are not able to give birth to children. I never imagined I'd ever write these ideas in a book, let alone would court controversy by saying so.

So it's particularly truth-defying that the LGBTQIA+ movement not only demands that you reject the immutability of sex despite the hard genetic and anatomical basis for it, but also demands that you do so *while also embracing the immutability of sexual orientation*—despite lack of *any* genetic, anatomical, biological, physical, or otherwise observable basis for saying so.*

My point is simple: you can't believe both of these things at the same time if you claim to adopt a belief system in accordance with logic or science. If it's a religion, you're free to believe whatever you want. But you're *not* free to force everyone else to bow down to your religion. And in modern America, the most oppressive religions of all are the ones that masquerade in the garb of science or reason.

"THIS IS ABOUT RIGHTS"

The gay rights movement began as one that, on its own terms, stood up to a tyranny of the majority. The legal toolkit afforded by the Fourteenth Amendment of the U.S. Constitution and the civil rights laws are designed to protect against a tyrannical majority denying the rights of minority groups—and eventually formed the basis for marriage equality in America. But that is now perverted into something else altogether: in the name of protecting against a tyranny of the majority, we have created a *new* tyranny of the minority. And not a large minority, but a *fringe* minority.

It turns out the so-called struggle for "transgender rights" isn't really about rights at all. It's a new form of vindictive *oppression* against the majority of Americans. Without a single new law being passed to protect "trans rights," I'll wait for a good answer to the question of what a gay or transgender person *can't* do today that a straight or cisgender person can. I haven't heard one yet.

Instead the demands relate to other affirmative claims they wish to

---

* *I'm not the only person to make this observation. I'd like to credit Douglas Murray in his insightful book* The Madness of Crowds *for making a similar argument. It was arguably braver of him to say than me, because he's gay.*

make. Men do not have an inherent "right" to compete in women's sports, any more than a heavyweight boxer has a "right" to compete in a lightweight class. Yet that's a central fixation of the modern "trans rights" movement.

There's no question that this hurts women, and not only because biological males have an unfair physical advantage over them. As Riley Gaines, a former teammate of University of Pennsylvania swimmer Lia Thomas, has pointed out, it also makes for some horrific locker room situations. As Gaines recently told Bill Maher, Thomas would walk around naked before meets, waving "her" penis around for the other women to see. She also noted that at the time of the national championships, Thomas was still actively pursuing sex with women.[8] In less insane times, this might be called voyeurism. We would be talking about the rights of the young women rather than the single biological male looking to rack up medals and trophies by arguably exploiting a broken system.

Or take the case of "transgender rights" to use the bathroom of the opposite sex. The inherent biological differences between men and women have always created a legally permissible distinction between men's and women's restrooms. Aside from basic logic, there are good reasons for this. The most important is safety. One need only conduct a cursory Google search to find examples of transgender women—biological males—who have entered bathrooms and assaulted biological women, using their large stature and superior physical strength to inflict maximum damage. It happened in Oklahoma in 2022.[9] And Wyoming in 2017.[10] And Virginia in 2021.[11] Recently, an organization called the Utah Gay-Straight Coalition compiled a list of just some of the known sexual assaults that have occurred in bathrooms.[12] A shocking amount of these have involved young, vulnerable girls.

This brings me to the most egregious cases of all—the intentional foisting of the "transgender rights" agenda onto children. Gender dysphoria is, for the rare few people who suffer from it, a great source of suffering indeed. Yet it's a *psychological* condition, one that deserves compassion and treatment. The new "trans rights" agenda rejects the treatment of this condition because of its refusal to acknowledge it as a condition of suffering. As a consequence, they create even more of it.

During my presidential campaign, I met two young women who are now in their twenties. During their earlier teenage years, both went through periods of psychological insecurity and lost their self-confidence and sense of who they were—among other things, a loss of self-confidence about their gender identity. Yet they didn't get the psychological help they needed. Pharmacotherapy and surgery intervened instead. Both received medicines that blocked their puberty. Both received double mastectomies—serious surgeries that involved cutting off both of their breasts. One of them received a full hysterectomy—a removal of her uterus—*as a teenager.*

Both women now deeply regret the decisions they made—or more precisely, the decisions that were made *for* them, since they were minors—and can't do anything to change it. They will anatomically and biologically never be the same again. Affirming a kid's confusion isn't compassion. It's a new form of cruelty.

This is remarkable because compassion for children is the general argument made against new laws that prevent the use of puberty blockers or transgender surgery on minors. It's not a strictly partisan matter. In Ohio, Governor Mike DeWine, a Republican, vetoed a bill that would have restricted gender-affirming care for minors. In Arkansas, then-governor Asa Hutchinson did the same thing. In May 2023, three Democrats in Texas broke with their party to support a state bill that would ban hormone therapies, puberty blockers, and surgeries in children.[13]

But it turns out that most children who go through so-called "gender-affirming care" are psychologically no more satisfied or better off after receiving their chemical intervention or surgery than beforehand—because, just like the two women whom I met during the campaign, they were going through an independently challenging period in their lives.

"THERE AREN'T *REALLY* TWO GENDERS"

What's the best argument for the other side? Often, deflection. I frequently heard people during the campaign challenge me, as if I didn't learn it in my freshman-year genetics course, by arguing that there *aren't* really just two biological sexes in the first place. It turns out that there *are* a very small number of people who are biologically "intersex." These are medical conditions unrelated to mental health or gender dysphoria. For example, certain people are born with two X chromosomes *and* a Y chromosome. They're XXY, which means they suffer from Klinefelter syndrome. Others are born with one X chromosome and two Y chromosomes; they suffer from Jacobs syndrome. These are part of a broad class of medical disorders known as chromosomal abnormalities, which occur for sex chromosomes just as they do for other chromosomes—such as trisomy 18, the occurrence of three copies of chromosome 18 (rather than just two), which manifests as Down syndrome. Most chromosomal abnormalities are terminal in utero, but the few that allow a fetus to survive through birth result in those born with these syndromes. Note that these genetic abnormalities are extremely rare. Taken together, they affect only about 3 to 5 percent of the population.

Fine. This is true and deserves to be acknowledged. As a technical matter, it's not actually true that "there are two genders" because there are not just two "sexes," if you count those who suffer from these ultrarare chromosomal abnormalities and related diseases. But that proves the core point: there is a genetic basis for gender, and that gender is determinable, and objectively true at birth. And equally importantly, everything except XY and XX is a *pathology*. A medical disorder. And transgenderism is no different.

Further, the fact that there may be *variability* in gender beyond XX and XY does not imply *mutability*. Imagine that you made the highly uncontroversial point that a person's eye color was genetically determined and immutable, and that there are three eye colors: blue, brown, and hazel.

Then assume someone pointed out that there are actually more eye colors than blue, brown, and hazel because, for example, some people have heterochromia (one blue eye and one brown eye) and other people may have whitish eyes due to albinism.

That may all be well and good, but it hardly means that someone who is born with blue eyes can identify as someone with brown eyes. Or that such a person isn't "really" someone with blue eyes. Or that a child who claims they were meant to be born with brown eyes should be given eyedrops to permanently change their eye color. Or that taxpayers should be forced to foot the bill for "eye-color-affirming care." It doesn't really make any sense.

"GENDER IS A SOCIAL CONSTRUCT"

The more forceful argument for the other side states that while *sex* may be biologically hardwired, gender doesn't have to be. Gender can be a social construct that supervenes on sex. Why draw the distinction? Because in a civil and respectful society, every person deserves to be acknowledged in the manner they *prefer* to be acknowledged. Just as you deserve the dignity of being called by your own name and not the one that someone else chooses for you, you deserve the dignity of being addressed and treated as the gender that you identify with, not the one someone else decides is yours.

That argument sounds compelling, but only to a point. As a civil society, we patently *reject* the unilateral latitude of every individual to claim to be a member of a particular group, when it has implications for the identity and perspective of other members of that particular group. Take the question of race. Suppose a white person *calls* himself black and expects to be treated as such. If most black people in a particular community flat-out reject that notion and don't treat the white person as such, I don't think most people who disagree with me on the transgender question would argue that the white person deserves to be "acknowledged" as black—even if, as a legal matter, he couldn't be turned away from an all-black fraternity party.

The alternative reaction, I suspect, would be compassionate concern for the white person's well-being. It is certainly plausible that if a white person were suffering from a delusion that he was the reincarnation of Malcolm X or a black prophet due to schizophrenia or some other mental illness, his claims would be met not with offense or hostility, but with concern. Depending on how well they know the man, they may try to get him help, perhaps a psychiatric evaluation, or contact family members, or determine whether he has been taking his medications. But the fact that his delusion is sincerely held, and that some members of the black community would be understanding and compassionate, does not mean that black people would (or should) agree with the white person's claim to blackness. To be sure, they would likely still oppose that man leading the local chapter of the NAACP (à la Rachel Dolezal) or claiming eligibility for minority set-asides. And with good reason! That person is not actually black! Even if he strongly, sincerely believes he is. And if he resists treatment and continues to demand the "privileges" anyway—including access to culture spaces created and reserved for those of a particular social group to which he does not belong—those efforts are likely to be met with irritation and ultimately offense.

It's not so different when female competitors in sports—the likes of Riley Gaines—find Lia Thomas's adoption of a woman's identity offensive. By parallel logic, Lia Thomas is not only not a woman, it means Lia is arguably a *misogynist*. Just as we acknowledge that it's not solely up to the white man to call himself black, and that black people in his community do have some claim on the matter of the white man's race, so too do female athletes have a say in the identity of a man who claims to be a woman for the purpose of competing in women's sports. It turns out that any civil society *does* adopt limitations on the monopoly of an individual to decide which group identity he can adopt for himself—when it implicates the identity or experience of other members of that group.

It's offensive when the white man in the hypothetical paints his face black, wears dreadlocks, and speaks in Ebonics—for the same reason that many women find it offensive when transgender surgeries reinforce the preconceived notions of what types of lips or breasts a true "woman" is supposed to have. The central premise of the equal rights movement for women was that there are many ways to be a woman, just as those who advocate for true racial equality embrace that there are many ways to be black.

One such woman came to one of my campaign events to publicly challenge me on what she had heard from secondhand sources regarding my "hostile" views toward LGBTQ persons. She had a crew cut. She wore traditionally "masculine" clothing, all the way down to the style of her eyeglasses. She initially started interrupting my speech, and when I gave her the microphone—as was my standard practice with protestors—she excoriated me for my disrespect toward the LGBT community. She mounted a lengthy monologue about her challenges of growing up as a lesbian woman in southwest Iowa. After I retook the microphone, I told her that I had nothing against her or the way she wanted to live her life—but that it was another matter to try to alter how men and women use bathrooms, or how women compete with men in sports, or —

She interrupted me: *Wait, what did you say?* she asked.

I repeated the last thing I said: I don't think that men should be allowed to compete with women in women's sports, period.

She then paused for a long moment. I couldn't tell if she was going to lash out at me, or turn around and just walk out. Instead, she said in response: "Wait a minute, I agree with you on that." The audience again erupted in applause; she came up to the front. We slapped each other a high five, and we had a photo and a drink together after the event. Turns out she was a veteran who had served in the army. We ended up talking about various improvements that our country needs to make to the Department of Veterans Affairs. Speaking with her was a reminder—one of many that I got throughout the campaign—that in general, people are not crazy, and that we tend to agree on more things than we disagree on. The important thing is that we talk to each other and refuse to allow certain topics to be taken out of the realm of free and open debate.

"THIS DOESN'T HURT ANYONE"

While much of the debate often surrounds men competing in women's sports, there is one place where opportunistic transgenderism is far more dangerous: prison. It's true that female college athletes may be more sympathetic (certainly more innocent) victims of transgendered takeover of previously female spaces, but the consequences for female inmates are far more dire. Take the case of Stephen Wood in the UK.[14] Wood was already a convicted pedophile, but now he was back in jail again. This time he was being held on new charges that he had raped a woman and stabbed a neighbor after his previous release. And something else had changed. Now he wore a blond wig, called himself "Karen," and argued that he should be held in a women's prison. The politically correct bureaucratic elites couldn't disagree. Their hands were tied. *He bought the wig*, they must have thought to themselves, palms facing the ceiling. *There is literally nothing else we can do.* So they allowed Wood to be held in the female ward—where he went on to sexually assault multiple additional women.

This is not an isolated incident. Since California enacted its gender-affirming prison law in 2017, claims of transgenderism among inmates are up 237 percent. Progressives have all kinds of explanations—hate-filled transphobic police officers are profiling transgendered people, trumping up charges and throwing them in jail at higher rates; transgendered folks lack social and economic support and so are disproportionately forced to resort to a life of crime, etc.—but what if the answer were far more obvious? Claims of transgenderism among inmates is rising not because trans-gendered people are committing (or accused of) more crimes, but because people committing (or accused of) crimes are increasingly claiming to be transgendered. Duh. Being held in a women's prison has lots of benefits. It is typically much calmer, less violent, more relaxed. There's more freedom. Fewer lockdowns. There are also a lot more vulnerable women around to rape, if that's your cup of tea.

People respond to incentives. Criminals do too. Progressive elites who refuse to even entertain the possibility that someone could be lying about something so sacrosanct as their gender identity, the pearl-clutchers who believe that such a false claim is so morally abhorrent that no person— even a convicted criminal—would be willing to desecrate such a holy principle they hold so dear, are suffering from far grander delusions than a man who believes he is female. As a representative democracy, the Ameri-can body politic depends on our elected representatives to be our eyes and ears, to make policy judgments for the good of the electorate based on sound reasoning and solid facts. Yet when it comes to transgender policies, progressives (and sometimes even so-called conservatives) legislate based on willful blindness, refusing to see the truth in plain sight, lodging fin-gers in their ears to avoid listening to the cries of victims harmed by the policies they embrace.

Female athletes and inmates are among the most directly affected, but all of us suffer, particularly when the time comes to pay the bill. Prisoners are entitled to have taxpayers pay for sex-change surgeries (maybe even as a matter of constitutional right, as activists claim it is cruel and unusual punishment for a transgendered inmate to be denied an all-expenses-paid gender transition). But innocent children have no constitutional right to dental care. That means that a single mother who works two fast-food jobs to make ends meet has money taken out of her paycheck every week so that Lil' Shorty can become No Shorty, while cavities rot her chil-dren's teeth. And prisoners aren't the only ones on the government dole.

Transgender employees may also be entitled to have their surgeries and hormone-replacement therapies covered by insurance (there are lawsuits pending about whether denial of transgender care is gender discrimination, but even if there is no legal right, the fact is that most insurance covers it anyway), even as employers (both state and private) are cutting coverage for what could very well be lifesaving diabetes treatments. In a reality where there are limited resources (which, admittedly, is not the world in which most progressives live), how as a society do we decide how to allocate scarce medical care?

Here's the crazy part: if you asked that question of transgender activists, they would say that those scarce health care resources should be used to treat a medical condition *that they deny is a medical condition at all.*

Many transgender organizations strongly advocate for the complete removal of gender dysphoria from the *DSM* because according to them transgenderism is not a psychiatric or medical condition; it is a social construct (or, perhaps, normal variability within the human population).[15] But if being transgender not a medical problem—or, in their view, a problem at all—then why should medical insurance pay for treatment?

The internal incoherence is even more incomprehensible when one considers that a major tenet of the transgender movement is that someone's transition is no less valid just because an individual chose not to undergo surgery. In other words, an XY who "is a woman" is no less a woman just because she has testicles and other male anatomy. Surgery is an individual choice, and deciding whether or not to go under the knife has no bearing on how "legitimate" one's transition is. But if that's true, then even as a matter of social construct (setting aside the fact that there is no medical necessity if transgenderism is no longer a medical issue), the desire to remove traditionally "male" anatomy is a mere preference (though admittedly a strong one for some people). In that case, by the transgender movement's own principles, the removal of non-traditionally-conforming body parts is purely cosmetic.

That means insurance shouldn't pay for it. Transgenderists know this. So the smart ones only soft-pedal their "opposition" to the psychiatric diagnosis. But reluctantly agreeing to have "gender dysmorphia" stay in the *DSM* only to ensure insurance coverage is essentially fraud. It's no different from women who would like government- or employer-funded liposuction from creating a new diagnosis for "large waist dysmorphia" and then insisting that insurance foot the bill. Either being transgender is a mental illness (in which case there is at least an argument that insurance should cover treatment, although whether the treatment should be mental-health-based counseling or surgical intervention is an open question) or it is not. But they can't have it both ways.

"THIS IS ABOUT BIGOTRY"

The earnest version of the underlying debate is really about compassion versus cruelty. Proponents of each side of the broader transgender debate believe they're on the side of compassion, and the other is on the side of cruelty. No amount of argument will persuade a committed soldier on the other side of the debate, because reason wasn't the foundation for their views in the first place. But I think a certain demonstration of empathy, without compromising on the need to protect children from physical or chemical intervention or the integrity of women's sports, ends up going a long way.

One of the biggest surprises of my time on the campaign came from none other than the mainstream press. During the campaign cycle, TV networks "embed" young reporters with major presidential campaigns to attend every campaign event and press conference and more generally cover the candidate. I saw these reporters nearly every day for more than a year.

One of these embeds was a reporter from a major news organization. Let's call her Kori. Kori was particularly hardworking—never missing an event and always jumping at the chance to ask a question. Kori would frequently, and respectfully, challenge me on the issue of gender identity, particularly on my view that transgenderism is a mental health disorder.

At one event in eastern Iowa at a packed bar of fifty people or so in the late afternoon, I had fielded some particularly animated questions about transgenderism being foisted onto children in schools across the state and the country. There were a number of parents in the room who were understandably frustrated and publicly voiced their concerns, which encouraged even more to follow. For my part, I responded without caveat that transgenderism is a mental health condition and needs to be treated as such—which drew raucous applause from the audience. After that event, Kori chased me down in the parking lot and asked to have a one-on-one conversation as I walked to the bus.

It was an unusual move, because usually the "press embeds" got to speak with me in the context of a press gaggle, or else we'd just see them at a future event. Yes, occasionally there were the overaggressive hostile reporters who tried to scream a gotcha question at you to capture you in a bad light—random reporters from CNN or NBC who might shout "what do you make of President Trump's comments calling his political opponents 'vermin' today," when it turns out that that's not even what Trump said—but Kori wasn't one of them. To the contrary, her reporting had called balls and strikes fairly throughout the campaign, even when critical of me, but hadn't been unnecessarily biased or attempted to drive a particular narrative. Kori was earnest.

So when she approached me in an uncharacteristic manner, even though we were running late to an event in Davenport that required some time to reach in a cumbersome bus, I took the time to talk to her in the parking lot. I paused and saw her eyes half-filled with tears, so I stepped aside from the path of the stream of my team and press exiting the event, and gestured to my team to give me a second alone. My press secretary looked a little skeptical—by that point in the campaign, we'd learned our lesson to record every conversation I had with a member of the press—but I gave her a nod suggesting that this one would be all right. It turned out the conversation Kori wanted to have was a personal one.

"I've really enjoyed getting to know you, and especially Apoorva and the kids, this year. But I just have to ask you: What gives you the confidence that there are really just two genders?" Kori asked me, with a slight tremble in her voice.

Yes, I was talking on the record to a mainstream reporter who was recording what I said. Tricia, my senior advisor who led communications for the campaign, noticed that and started to approach Kori and me to follow our standard protocol of recording every conversation I had with a member of the press corps—a lesson we had learned the hard way after having walked into some traps earlier in the year. But I gave Tricia a brief glance to suggest that she should hang back. She gestured with her eyes to double-check that I was sure, and I nodded. This wasn't really a conversation with the press. It was a personal conversation with someone whom I had grown to respect as a person, and—though she's never said it in so many words—I believe had grown to respect my family and me too. And Kori was clearly upset.

I explained my view that it started with biology, in the same way I did in my on-air interview with NBC's Chuck Todd. If you have two X chromosomes, with a female reproductive system, you're a woman. If you have an X and a Y chromosome, with a male reproductive system, you're a man. Period.

But then it hit me: Kori wasn't feigning indignation or manufacturing a gotcha question. This wasn't actually a *debate*. She was talking to me because she identified as nonbinary herself. She felt hurt by my comments, not sanctimoniously on some unknown other person's behalf, but on her own behalf. She was hurt not because she detested me, but because—I think—she respected me. For the entire campaign, I viewed her as a young woman. She was black, or at least appeared to be, but had a boyish haircut and a deeper-than-normal voice for a woman of her age, in her early twenties just out of college, and was consistently a little more hard-working and a lot more thoughtful than her peers in the same profession.

My team was giving me gestures to wrap it up and move on to the next event, but this was an important conversation. I wasn't going to have the time to debate the points logically, nor was the debate really the conversation we needed to have. Kori was frustrated by my response, but she didn't really counter either.

So I asked Kori about her own identity. She said she identified as non-binary. I asked her when she landed at that realization, and she said it was late in high school. When I asked what was different about her experience relative to a young woman who discovers different sexual preferences than most of her peers, she paused and became pensive. She didn't have a ready answer, and I didn't intend to push her on the point either.

We instead shifted to a conversation about her family. She grew up in a single-parent household in Baltimore, to a single black mother, and her father had ended up in prison for many years, which strained her relationship, though it sounded like she had worked to rekindle it after her father got out. She didn't come from the kind of background where you'd predict she'd graduate from college, much less go on to become a journalist who—at least according to this former presidential candidate—was among the very best at what she did at a major news network. Having seen her work ethic and quality of work, I would hire her in the future if given the chance.

Yet here she was, waking up at the crack of dawn in a state that was far from the inner city of Baltimore, where she grew up, or cosmopolitan New York City, where she lived now, making it to most events slightly ahead of me to set up her camera.

We didn't really come to much of a resolution, other than to smile and politely agree we would continue the conversation. It turns out I've seen Kori a number of times since then. She's the only press embed I've regularly stayed in touch with after the campaign ended. When I visited with *The Breakfast Club* for a podcast in New York City—hosted by two left-leaning black hosts who had criticized me for much of the campaign—I called Kori and invited her to join me backstage, not as a member of the press, but as a friend. She came along and my intention had been to finish the conversation we began in Iowa, but it turns out we just ended up talking about her getting a new apartment and the new beat that her employer had assigned her after I'd dropped out of the campaign.

There can be unity when there isn't uniformity, Rev. Martin Luther King Jr. once said. Maybe Kori and I will finish our discussion from that parking lot in Iowa one day. Maybe we won't. But when I remember my relationship with Kori, my debate with her on transgenderism certainly won't be the most important part.

FIVE TRUTHS

1. If you have two X chromosomes, you're a woman; if you have an X and a Y chromosome, you're a man.
2. The modern LGBTQIA+ movement adopts two contradictory claims at once: first, that the sex of the person you're attracted to is hardwired at birth (even though there is no "gay gene"), and second, that your own sex can be totally fluid over the course of your life (even though there is a definitive sex chromosome).
3. The fact that there are extremely rare genetic abnormalities where people are born with three sex chromosomes (XXY or XYY) does not change the fact that there are two biological sexes. This is a red herring to the modern transgender debate.
4. Gender dysphoria is a mental health condition. Affirming a child's gender confusion is not compassion. It's cruelty—because it often leads to greater dissatisfaction, depression, and the spread of gender dysphoria to other children in the same school or environment.

5. Transgender people can and should enjoy the right to live freely
without persecution. That's an entirely different matter from
indoctrinating children with modern gender theory at a young age,
permitting genital mutilation and chemical castration of minors, or
requiring women to compete with men in competitive sports.

5

THERE ARE THREE BRANCHES OF U.S. GOVERNMENT, NOT FOUR

"Can you please stop saying 'administrative state'? People tune out when you say it."

That sage advice came from Steve Moore, the famed economist who had invited me to speak to a group of policy wonks during the early phases of my campaign. A few weeks later, I got an unprompted call from Charlie Kirk, the founder of Turning Point USA, who isn't known for mincing words. "Man, you really need to stop saying 'administrative state.' It puts people to sleep."

Steve, Charlie, and I were on the same side of the policy question: the proliferation of three-letter federal agencies staffed by unelected bureaucrats who write endless regulations is an existential threat to the United States of America. But it's an issue that *bores* most voters. It sounds esoteric, like something that doesn't affect their everyday lives. Yet in the modern era of twisted American politics, it turns out the more mundane a topic sounds, the more you should pay attention—because it was probably *designed* to bore you into submission.

The other chapters of this book deal with the future direction of policy and culture in America. By contrast, this chapter is about the *procedure* of how our government actually functions. It's about the basic rules of the road.

And it's arguably the most important.

THE BASIC PROBLEM

The government exercises power in two main ways: by issuing binding edicts and carrying them out with force. Our constitutional republic ensures these powers are separated to prevent tyranny. The U.S. Constitution divides these duties among three branches: the legislative and judicial branches create and interpret laws, while the executive branch enforces them.

Take tax law, for example. Congress sets tax rates, federal courts interpret tax rules, and the Internal Revenue Service (IRS), part of the executive branch, enforces these laws. Similarly, Congress sets standards for drug approvals, courts interpret them, and the Food and Drug Administration (FDA) enforces compliance.

Ideally, this separation of powers keeps our government balanced.

In reality, the modern administrative state operates differently. Philip Hamburger, a Columbia Law School professor, compares this to "off-road driving." While the Constitution outlines proper lawmaking paths, the administrative state takes detours. As Hamburger says, "to leave the roads laid out by the Constitution can be exhilarating, at least for those in the driver's seat," with the government in control.

Today, most binding edicts come from the executive branch, not Congress or the courts. These regulations function as laws but bypass the constitutional process. This administrative state issues binding edicts directly. Debates on policies like abortion, gun control, and taxes overshadow the crucial issue of how these policies are enacted. The real question isn't about "where the government is heading, but how it drives."

This might seem like a legal technicality, but it strikes at the heart of the American Revolution. Our system is built on elected officials running the government. In a republic, citizens elect leaders to create laws; in a monarchy, subjects follow edicts without any say.

Despite our divisions, most Americans—regardless of race or political affiliation—value self-governance. Yet our country doesn't operate this way today. Although theoretically governed by three coequal branches with checks and balances, much political power is delegated to actors outside these branches, escaping the Founders' intended system.

This "shadow government" of unelected bureaucrats creates rules that affect everyone. These bureaucrats can't be voted out by citizens or fired by elected leaders. In the past, unelected rulers were kings; today they are technocrats in Washington, D.C. The threat to liberty remains the same.

This isn't a conspiracy theory. Lobbyists and unelected federal agency bureaucrats draft laws, often handed to Congress via the White House. Many Congress members pass these laws without reading them. Once signed into law, the real lawmaking begins through "rulemaking" by executive branch agencies. This creates a web of over 100,000 federal regulations affecting everyday Americans, made by unelected officials in a process unrecognized by the Constitution. If such a process had been proposed at the 1789 Constitutional Convention, it would have been dismissed as a bad joke.

Today, however, it's a sobering reality.

CASE STUDY OF BUREAUCRATS GONE WILD: THE SEC

Take the SEC—the Securities and Exchange Commission—the agency supposedly responsible for protecting investors from abuse. Our system of checks and balances goes to great lengths to separate those who write the rules from those who enforce them, and to separate both of those actors from the judges who interpret them. But just like at most government agencies, that's not how it works at the SEC.

Some of the most storied cases pursued by the SEC involve high-profile instances of insider trading—illegally using material nonpublic information about a company to buy and sell stocks. Yet it turns out that Congress never actually passed a law that bans insider trading. In fact, there is no law that even bothers to define it.

Instead it's all governed by *rules* written by the SEC, pursuant to a general federal statute that—in its famously broad Section 10b(5)—simply bans committing fraud on investors. Countless cases have landed in the Supreme Court opining on whether a particular set of facts constituted insider trading, including colorful cases of an enterprising printer figuring out what mergers were about to be announced, to an individual who was contacted by a whistleblower to expose a company's fraud. As the scope of infractions has increased, the Supreme Court has slapped the wrist of SEC officials who went too far in pushing cases against people who didn't really violate the law. Even in cases where the Supreme Court upheld convictions, dissenting judges often argue that no law had actually been broken. If even judges can't agree after the fact about whether an esoteric financial regulation had been violated, should an ordinary citizen go to jail or bear severe legal consequences for the action in question?

An easy fix would be to clarify the law itself. In fact, Congress has from time to time been pressed to consider a ban on insider trading altogether—something most Americans agree with. But there's been one curious constituency that has consistently opposed it. You might think it's the hedge fund lobbying association, but it turns out it's none other than the SEC itself.

On its face, this should be puzzling. The SEC is aggressive in trying to punish insider trading, yet there's no statute that expressly bans the very action they seek to punish. When Congress endeavors to create one, the SEC frets instead of rejoicing. That's because their top concern isn't actually combating insider trading, but rather expanding the scope of power they're able to exercise. If the elected representatives in *Congress* were the ones to define what did or didn't constitute a crime, that means the unelected bureaucrats at the SEC could no longer do it themselves. That makes the agency less relevant. And if there's one thing that administrative agencies do well, it's preserving and growing their existing authority. Like any biological organism, the chief goal is self-preservation.

It turns out that *most* binding edicts issued by the SEC were never enshrined in the law by Congress. An agency that is supposed to *enforce* the law ends up just making up laws on the fly—and then enforces *those* laws instead, by simply calling them "rules." In recent years, the SEC has doled out hundreds of millions of dollars in fines to financial institutions across the country—in one case, a staggering $250 million to JPMorgan Chase—for failing to stop their employees from using "off-channel communications," such as their personal phones, for communicating about any matter relating to business, although the bank refused to admit or deny any wrongdoing.[1] To be clear, that's *not* a penalty for individuals using their personal phones to commit crimes and then hiding it—but simply a penalty for the very act of using their personal phones *at all*, regardless of whether they were violating the law by doing so.

The justification for the rule is that the SEC can more easily detect wrongdoing at financial services firms if it has centralized access to all business-related communications. But that's true of *any* government surveillance effort. The Fourth Amendment wasn't designed to make it more convenient for the government to collect information from individuals; to the contrary, it was designed with the explicit goal of making it *less* convenient for the government to do so.

The Fourth Amendment protects us against unlawful searches and seizures by the government. It guarantees a substantive right to privacy against government surveillance, an idea enshrined in America's culture to this day. Congress could never pass a statute expressly outlawing the use of SMS text messages or WhatsApp by employees of entire sectors of the economy. Civil libertarians both on the right and the left would cry foul, and for good reason. It's an affront to the Fourth Amendment, and there would be instant constitutional challenges. It's also an affront to our intuitive understanding of freedom in America, and the public backlash would be even more swift than the court cases. Any Democrat or Republican who voted for such a law would be at risk of getting voted out of office quickly—which explains why Congress hasn't done it.

But the SEC has done exactly that via administrative rulemaking. It's using a backdoor mechanism to establish private-sector surveillance that Congress could not achieve through the front door.

Crucially, the problem here isn't *just* that there are millions of agency rules like this one that bind citizens and never went through the constitutionally ordained lawmaking process—though that alone spits in the face of the Constitution. It's even worse than that: the "rules" passed by these agencies are precisely the ones that never would have passed public muster if Congress had debated them in the open. It's not just a constitutional foot fault. It's an intentionally designed betrayal of the lawmaking process.

This may sound like flagrantly lawless behavior—because it is. The existence of the administrative state is an affront to our Constitution that our Founders never countenanced. The bureaucrats in the administrative state treat the actual laws that bind *them* as pesky inconveniences, rather than properly viewing the enforcement of the law itself as their raison d'être in the first place.

In an ultimate irony, it turns out that many SEC employees themselves regularly use off-channel communications outside of their government email addresses to avoid sunshine laws and Freedom of Information Act transparency procedures that otherwise would allow the public to see their communications. This was highlighted in a reverse lawsuit, *United States v. SEC*, in which it was alleged that SEC employees used personal devices and encrypted messaging apps to evade transparency requirements.[2] It's no coincidence that the very bureaucrats who disregard the Constitution in their manner of passing laws are also the ones who fail to follow the actual *laws* that constrain their own behaviors.

Once you see it, you can't unsee it. It's pervasive. The simplest litmus test for unlawful agency rulemaking is to ask the basic question of whether a majority of publicly elected representatives in Congress could have ever conceivably voted for that rule. If the answer is no, that means the rule probably isn't just unlawful—it's dangerous.

Try that litmus test on a different SEC rule—one that applies to settlements reached by private parties with the SEC.

Suppose your company was persecuted by the SEC for the high crime of failing to stop your employees from using their personal phones at work (which is itself, as previously discussed, not actually banned by law but only by fiat from the SEC). Instead of going through the arduous process of contesting the SEC's enforcement action against you, and taking the risk that the SEC might use its regulatory authority to try to put you out of business, you might choose to settle your case with them by paying a financial penalty. In fact this is what *most* businesses charged by the SEC choose to do.

Well, in that case, there's another SEC rule that functions like a gag order: it says that anyone who settles with the SEC *cannot criticize the agency's enforcement action*. If the First Amendment was designed to secure one right above all, it was the right of a U.S. citizen to be able to openly criticize the U.S. government. That's what makes someone a citizen of a republic, not the subject of a ruler. Yet we now have unelected bureaucrats issuing edicts *outside* of the process of lawmaking that legally bind private citizens from criticizing those bureaucrats.

Apply the basic litmus test: Would publicly elected representatives in Congress ever pass a law that applies legal penalties to citizens who reach a financial settlement with a government agency from ever criticizing that government agency? Of course not. It would be every bit of an affront to the First Amendment as a ban on the use of SMS text messages would represent an affront to the Fourth Amendment. The public outcry would create grave political risk to any congressman who tried. That's exactly why Congress hasn't done it—yet once again, that's exactly why the SEC has. The net result is a wide swath of private financial services businesses who were persecuted by an agency for a behavior that Congress never prohibited, and who are further unable to criticize that agency for doing so.

In sum, there are *two* basic constitutional violations at work here. The first is that agencies like the SEC are using the rulemaking process to issue binding edicts that Congress never passed. The second is the consolidation of legislative and executive power in one politically unaccountable body: the same agency that writes the rules is *also* the one that enforces them, which consolidates power in a single actor in a manner that the Framers of our Constitution never envisioned. For example, the SEC employs not just the bureaucrats who wrote the rules that ban the use of personal cell phones for business matters, but it *also* employs the bureaucrats who enforce those rules—via its own Enforcement Division.

This problem of consolidated power gets even worse. The same agency that writes the rules *and* enforces the rules is *also* the one that gets to interpret the rules—in the form of administrative law judges who sit within the agency itself. These "judges" interpret the SEC's rules to adjudicate disputes when an individual contests a fine the SEC has levied. This now becomes a total consolidation of executive, legislative, *and* judicial power—in one agency.

As it turns out, in over 90 percent of cases, the in-house administrative judges at an administrative agency rule in favor of the agency rather than the defendant, without any jury to moderate the outcome. One in-house SEC judge had a shocking 51-0 record of ruling for the agency, having never seen a single case in which the judge believed the accused should win. This should surprise no one.

These problems are by no means unique to the SEC. They pervade the *entire* administrative state, comprising more than four hundred agencies.

The people who staff these agencies were never elected to their positions. Ordinarily we think of ourselves as living in a country where the voting public gets to vote *out* the elected representatives who fail to serve them. That's certainly the country that our Founders thought they were setting into motion, markedly different from their experience as the colonial subjects of King George III. But the truth is—and this isn't something that any partisan Republican *or* Democrat really contests—the staff in the federal bureaucracy can't be voted out of their office, no matter how grossly they violate the spirit of our Constitution or the will of the electorate.

Now, I know I promised you at the start of this book that I would write in language appropriate for dinner-table conversation. But allow me to break that rule for a moment to analyze the *motives* of managerial actors in the administrative state.

DEFENDERS OF THE ADMINISTRATIVE STATE

Defenders of the status quo argue that the U.S. president still must *appoint* the leaders of each of these agencies, with the advice and consent of the U.S. Senate. Even though the heads of the FDA and SEC aren't *themselves* elected, the people who appoint them are.

This defense fails on two counts. First, it still fails to address the core separation-of-powers problem: the legislative branch is supposed to *make* the laws, whereas the executive branch of government is supposed to *enforce* the law. Our Framers designed a system in which the leaders of both were elected through the democratic process, but still further built in the need for dividing up which branches of government carried out its two central functions: who makes binding edicts versus who uses force to execute them. Even if agency heads were democratically elected, that still would not solve the problem regarding division of power.

The more practical problem is that it's a myth that the bureaucrats who write binding regulations are *really* accountable to the elected representatives at all. Most Americans assume that this means the representatives we elect to run the government—such as the president—can hire and fire those bureaucrats in these agencies if they do a poor job. Not quite. There are over four million federal bureaucrats, yet fewer than three thousand of them are actually able to be fired by the president—or even by cabinet-level secretaries in the U.S. government. That's because the remainder are protected by so-called "civil service protections" designed to shield them from politically motivated firings.

The basic logic of these rules is that we as a country don't want an apolitical career employee at FDA—whose daily job it is to make a decision about the safety risks of an investigational medicine—to be vulnerable to retaliation by a president who disagrees with that employee on the topic of, say, gun control or abortion. The justification for civil service protections is that technocrats shouldn't be subject to the vicissitudes of politics or the temperaments of politicians who come and go. That makes for poorer technical decisions, less stability for regulated private industry, and diminished trust in bureaucratic expertise—or so the argument goes.

But here's the problem: in the name of protecting technical experts from political retaliation, we have inadvertently created an entirely new class of politically *unaccountable* bureaucrats who can't be fired even for failing to do the very job that they're hired to do.

Suppose the president is elected after making a campaign promise to speed up the process of reviewing new medicines, with the goal of reducing prescription drug costs by introducing greater competition. If there's a career FDA employee who disagrees with *that* policy and continues reviewing investigational medicine applications at the same sluggish pace, the president should be able to fire him. But he can't. And even more shockingly, *neither can the FDA commissioner.* The civil service rules protect that employee from being fired other than "for cause"—which includes only the most egregious and often illegal behaviors such as stealing government property or being intoxicated on the job.

That's the shadow government in a nutshell—the millions of bureaucrats who were never elected to their positions exercising far greater political power than most elected representatives do.

Defenders of the status quo would argue that the decision by an FDA bureaucrat to review investigational drug applications more slowly—more "carefully"—isn't a political decision at all, but a technical one. This goes to the heart of the debate: most decisions made by the government are inherently political, yet the ones made by the bureaucracy are disguised in the veneer of technocracy. The description of a given scientific risk or medical benefit isn't a political decision, but the decision of how to weigh those risks against one another—or to weigh the cost and benefit of taking an extra year to assess a risk versus the system-wide increase in prescription drug costs as a consequence—is a decision grounded in *values*. The decision by a government actor of whether to prioritize speed and cost over reducing a small increment of risk is a political decision.

For better or worse, our nation was founded on the basic idea that these political decisions ultimately belong to the citizens of our nation—and the leaders we elect to represent us. That's what makes America great. That's what makes America *itself*.

But America is no longer itself. Not only do nearly four million federal bureaucrats escape all forms of political accountability, even as they defy the political will of the electorate. The way these agencies are structured today also violates the principle of separation of powers enshrined in our Constitution.

There's a temptation to view the entire project of the "deep state"—the class of politically unelected, unfireable bureaucrats who set the most important public policies—as pernicious in its intentions. Managerial bureaucrats cloistered in the backs of ugly government buildings, penning restrictive regulations, and doing so with impunity and no accountability to the public, naturally invites an angry reaction from those of us who see how things actually work.

But that anger risks clouding our discernment. It's not that bureaucrats subvert the democratic will of the people through their elected representatives because they want to screw us over. The real motivation of most bureaucrats is their elite *benevolence*—that their decisions may save us from the otherwise ill-fated decisions that an ordinary voting public might make for itself.

Many climate-change regulations—both via the regulatory state and the back door of the private sector—fit this description. The electorate doesn't support the requirement for public companies to have to disclose how much CO_2 they emit, and that's why the people who they elected never codified that into a statute.

The SEC did it through backdoor regulation instead, attempting to enact rules that would mandate new "climate risk disclosures" for every publicly traded company. The justification is that investors deserve to understand all material risks, but this is tautological because the SEC *already* requires companies to disclose, at behest of liability, all material risks. That means that if climate change were indeed a "material risk" for a particular company, that company would already be in violation of the law for failing to disclose that risk in their quarterly filings. Under the prior rules, it would be preposterous for the SEC to charge a publicly traded company like, hypothetically, Netflix for its failure to disclose climate change as a material risk factor. So it tried to do something even more preposterous: require public companies to disclose climate-change risk factors anyway, effectively admitting that climate change is *not* a material risk factor in the first place. Their counterparts at countless other agencies like the EPA have adopted similar tactics to backdoor-legislate the climate agenda (more on that shortly).

Crucially, it's *not* that they are subverting the will of the people because they're hostile to the people; it's because they believe that the people, if left entirely to govern themselves without elite supervision, will self-destruct . . . in this case, through self-immolation of the planet itself. That's why it needed to be done by bureaucratic rulemaking justified by irrelevant goals like "investor protection." If a company were as dishonest with the public as the SEC, they'd have been sued out of existence.

But it's worth taking the question seriously—of whether the public will *needs* to be overridden and even duped by experts from time to time. That was the view of Woodrow Wilson, the twenty-eighth president of the United States and godfather of the modern administrative state, who famously argued that "popular sovereignty" "embarrasse[d]" the nation, because it made it harder to achieve "executive expertness." He faulted the country for "trying to do too much by vote," particularly when those votes were cast by "ignorant negroes" or immigrants "from the south of Italy" who failed to possess "any initiative of quick intelligence." Better to leave the governance to the experts, to the elites.

The rise of the managerial class is really a form of modern monarchy, grounded in benevolence, just as it was in the old European aristocracy. As Philip Hamburger explains, the history of administrative law stretches back many centuries. "It is not a coincidence that administrative law looks remarkably similar to the sort of governance that thrived long ago in medieval and early modern England under the name of the 'prerogative.'" Just as the king had the royal prerogative to issue edicts and govern his subjects largely unchecked, so too does the administrative state operate with absolute, consolidated, extralegal power. Accordingly, while this sort of power "is said to be uniquely modern, [it] is really just the most recent manifestation of a recurring problem." And not just *a* recurring problem, but the very recurring problem that the Framers set out to prevent.

And *that's* why our Founders fought the American Revolution: to embark on the great American experiment, to determine whether a people could truly be trusted to govern themselves, rather than ruled by a group of monarchs or enlightened elites who knew best.

Our current administrative state is antithetical to these principles and ought to be rejected by citizens of every political persuasion. Republicans may hate the Department of Education, and Democrats may dislike rule-making by ICE, but no one wants their lives to be controlled by millions of shadow bureaucrats elected by no one and accountable only to themselves.

ORDINARY AMERICANS, NOT JUST CORPORATIONS, SUFFER BECAUSE OF REGULATORY OVERREACH

The people who suffer at the hands of these agencies aren't just the unsympathetic financial institutions, hedge funds, and corporations that the

SEC goes after. They're real people. Ordinary hardworking Americans who get caught up in the agency racket.

Take a case that was decided by the U.S. Supreme Court as this book went to print: *Loper Bright Enterprises v. Raimondo.*

One of the petitioners is Bill Bright. He spent forty years in the fishing industry, working his way up from a deckhand to a role in the engine room to the wheelhouse. He scrimped and saved to be able to purchase a boat of his own—an old, leaky ship he named the F/V *Defiance*, as an ode to the naysayers in Bill's life who doubted his ability to keep the vessel, much less his fledgling business, afloat. Three decades later, and Bill is the captain and owner of a successful herring fishery. His two sons have joined the family business, and Bill has since purchased a second boat. His wife and two daughters manage the family's restaurant, which serves fresh-caught seafood straight from Bill's ships.

A new initiative from one of the hundreds of federal agencies you've never heard of—the National Marine Fisheries Service, or NMFS—now threatens to take all that away. By statute, the NMFS can require fishing vessels to host "onboard monitors"—essentially, federal regulators who accompany the fishermen on their voyages to ensure they are engaging in responsible fishing practices and otherwise complying with the agency's regulations. But then the agency began to run out of money. It couldn't pay all the salaries for all these onboard monitors aboard all these ships. And it knew that Congress was unlikely to open the federal pocketbook to shell out more cash. So instead it passed a regulation forcing fishermen to foot the monitors' salaries instead.

The salary for such a plush federal agency position is more than you might expect. Onboard monitors can make over seven hundred dollars a day, often more than the ship's captain himself. That can shave up to 20 percent off a vessel's total revenue, rendering the entire business unprofitable. That's more likely for smaller, family-run businesses, with smaller boats and smaller hauls. If the Supreme Court had ruled against Bright, the *Defiance* would likely have become the *Compliance*. And the extra weight of the regulations would almost surely have sunk the ship.

That would have been a grave threat to Bill Bright and fishermen like him. But it also would have been a threat to our democratic system of checks and balances. Think of it this way: the NMFS's new rule was akin to the IRS slapping you with an audit, and then politely informing you that, regardless of the outcome of the audit or whether you've done anything wrong, you'll now be billed for the auditor's salary for the privilege of the paper-trail patdown.

It's outrageous. But it also makes agencies even *less* accountable to the other, legitimate branches of government. Typically, one way Congress can rein in bad agency behavior is by cutting funding. Congress, after all, supposedly has the "power of the purse strings" when it comes to the government fisc. But if agencies are allowed to charge regulated entities for the privilege of being regulated—including forcing the people they regulate to fork over the agency staffers' salaries—agencies need not seek funding from Congress at all. The disease has freed itself from the host. Through creative self-funding, our ever-expanding federal bureaucracy can continue to feast unabated on whatever fees, surcharges, and taxes it decides to levy on all of us, every day, in ways both large and small.

None of this is constitutionally kosher. As Boston University law professor Gary Lawson has explained, "the modern administrative state is not merely unconstitutional; it is anti-constitutional. The Constitution was designed specifically to prevent the emergence of the kinds of institutions that characterize the modern administrative state."[3]

RAY OF HOPE: SUPREME COURT TO THE RESCUE

People have noted this problem for decades, and for years there wasn't really much that could be done about it—until recently. In 2022, the

Supreme Court delivered arguably its most important ruling in modern history: *West Virginia v. EPA*. The case nullified certain regulations issued by the U.S. Environmental Protection Agency (EPA), but if you take the court's reasoning seriously, it suggests that quite literally *most* federal regulations are unconstitutional. Yes, you read that correctly.

The case concerns the esoteric issue of the EPA's authority to regulate coal plants under the Clean Air Act. The EPA used that law as the justification to impose a wide range of ultraspecific requirements on coal plants—from the need to use specific scrubbers to the kinds of filters needed to reduce particle emissions. This effectively gave the EPA the authority to *put coal plants out of business* by setting emissions caps so low that no coal company would be able to comply. And that's exactly what the EPA set out to do.

If you're an environmental regulator, you view the elimination of coal plants as a good thing—without regard to the economic trade-offs of your action. The consequences are often dire. Shuttering coal plants means putting tens of thousands of miners out of work. Another cost is billions of dollars required to transition to alternative sources of energy, many of which lack the abundance or ability to fulfill the bare minimum needs of baseload power generation in the United States.* This translates to trillions in lost GDP and higher energy costs.

These questions may not matter to the EPA, but they certainly *do* matter to everyday American citizens who are adversely impacted—yet lack any ability to vote out the policymakers who were responsible for doing it to them. Thankfully the Supreme Court stepped in and nullified the regulation. The kind of policy matter the EPA had taken on—the kind of "major

---

* *Baseload power refers to the minimum level of consistent and reliable electricity that must be supplied to meet basic demand. It is typically provided by power plants that operate continuously, such as coal, natural gas, nuclear, and some hydroelectric plants, to ensure a stable and uninterrupted supply of electricity.*

question" that has large economic implications—is almost always reserved for Congress itself. So if Congress couldn't muster enough votes to pass a law outlawing coal plants, the EPA couldn't do it by regulatory fiat either.

It is difficult to overstate the seismic importance of this ruling. If the EPA regulations at issue in this case were unconstitutional, that means that quite literally most federal regulations are likely unconstitutional as well—from the SEC to FDA to Federal Trade Commission (FTC) to the rest of the federal-regulatory alphabet soup.

The Supreme Court's recent ruling in *Loper Bright* will make substantive changes in this area. In that case, the court took aim at another core principle that has allowed the administrative state to insulate itself from accountability: the *Chevron* doctrine. This is an old and tragic Supreme Court case that held that, except for certain rare circumstances, federal courts must *defer* to an agency's interpretation of the law, including its own rulemaking capacity, so long as the agency jumps through certain procedural hoops.

The best-known of those procedural hoops is that before an agency issues binding edicts, it must go through a "notice and comment" period from the public. That means that any time an agency is considering the passage of a new rule, it must publish the draft rule in the Federal Register ("notice") and solicit feedback ("comment") from members of the public. The basic idea here is that even though our Framers believed that laws should be passed by democratically elected lawmakers, it was acceptable as a pragmatic alternative to empower bureaucrats to also issue legally binding edicts so long as the public is given the opportunity to participate in that rulemaking process.

It turns out this is a total farce. For starters, most Americans have never read the Federal Register or even heard of it. The parties who generally provide "comment" are professionals and lobbyists hired by massive corporations to do their bidding. And there's no requirement whatsoever that the federal agency change what it does in response to the comments that it receives—nor is there any mechanism for the public to hold those actors accountable.

In 2024, the Supreme Court decided the case of *SEC v. Jarkesy*, a ruling that, despite its limited publicity, had a significant impact. The Court's decision ended the practice of using in-house administrative law judges (ALJs) to impose civil penalties. The SEC had pursued an enforcement action against Jarkesy via its own in-house tribunal, rather than in federal courts. Jarkesy was found guilty and fined by the SEC.

However, after years of appeals, the Supreme Court ruled that the ALJ pathway violated Jarkesy's Seventh Amendment right to a trial by jury. The Court held that if a government agency seeks to fine you for violating its rules, you have a constitutional right to defend yourself in an actual courtroom, rather than in a tribunal run by the same agency that wrote the rules and investigated you. This decision would make our Founders proud.

In the same cycle, the Court also struck down the *Chevron* doctrine in the case of *Loper Bright v. Raimondo*. In *Chevron v. Natural Resources Defense Council* (1984), the Court had ruled that federal courts must defer to an agency's interpretation of the law as long as the agency followed certain procedures. This "*Chevron* deference" standard even applied to questions about the agencies' own rulemaking capacities. That ruling effectively replaced the legislative process laid out in our Constitution with a farcical administrative process for making rules and required federal courts to defer to agencies for their interpretation of the law.

In *Loper*, the six-justice majority got it right: "agencies have no special competence in resolving statutory ambiguities. Courts do." They effectively overturned the *Chevron* doctrine. Thanks to this ruling, federal courts must now ensure that agencies stay within statutory limits, without using statutory ambiguity as a smokescreen for administrative overreach.

The conditions have never been more ripe for dismantling the fourth branch of government, but this won't happen automatically. It requires both bottom-up litigation from private parties harmed by administrative overreach and, most importantly, strong action from a president willing to use the Supreme Court's recent rulings to permanently curtail the power of the administrative state.

THE PATH FORWARD

The problem of the administrative state is simple: the executive branch has reached far beyond its executive function to include legislative and even judicial power, without accountability. That means the actor who can fix this problem is the leader of the executive branch. That's the president. And here's the beginnings of how he could get the job done in a post-2022 legal landscape.

The president can appoint a czar who is accountable for permanently taming the administrative state. The czar could be the vice president, or it could be a "special advisor," or whatever. The title matters less than ensuring the czar sits above the bureaucracy and has the full backing of the president to tear down the fourth branch of government—by rescinding excess regulations, firing large numbers of bureaucrats, and shutting down redundant and unlawful administrative agencies.

The czar could embed a constitutionally trained lawyer in *every* administrative agency. That embedded lawyer would have a singular responsibility: apply the Supreme Court's major-questions standard to every federal regulation enacted by that agency. That list of regulations would then be presented to the president, who could, by executive action, rescind all of those regulations. This would pare most federal regulations and stimulate the economy by unshackling individuals and businesses from illicit regulations that were never passed through the constitutionally required process of lawmaking.

Like most conservatives, I'm skeptical of using presidential executive orders to accomplish what should be done via legislation. But to be clear, the presidential executive order *rescinding* those regulations would actually be the exact reverse of that—undoing the damage done by executive-crafted regulations that bypassed Congress in the first place. Crucially, a future president couldn't simply flip the switch and re-create the regulations that were rescinded by a previous one. He would have to go through Congress to create it from the ground up, even though a president *could* rescind the regulations without going through Congress. The beauty of this plan is that it's a one-way ratchet.

The antibureaucracy czar could use a similar approach for mass firings of federal bureaucrats as well. He could place an embed—this time, likely not a constitutional lawyer but a former CEO or reorganization expert—in each agency with the sole responsibility of identifying the minimal number of employees required at an agency for it to perform its more limited, constitutionally kosher function. The number of employees would be at least proportionately fewer to the number of regulations that were cut, but likely even more than that—because not only are fewer employees required to enforce fewer regulations, but the agency would also be *producing* fewer regulations in the first place if the scope of its regulatory authority were diminished.

Conventional wisdom holds that civil service protections stop the president—and even cabinet-level appointees—from firing federal workers. But civil service protections are not as strong as they're made out to be. It's true that more than 90 percent of federal agency employees have civil service protections. But the purpose of the law, originally passed in 1883, was to end the "spoils" system—that is, to prevent a newly elected president from rewarding supporters by granting them plum positions in the federal government. It essentially says that agency employees must be hired based on merit and cannot be fired based on their political beliefs. But it doesn't say that they can't be fired at all. To the contrary, the statute itself allows for mass layoffs—what it calls "reductions in force"—through which employees are entitled only to be retained in order of seniority.

The statute also empowers the president to "prescribe rules governing the competitive service" (5 U.S.C. 3302). This power is broad. Presidents from Harry Truman to Barack Obama have used this provision to amend the civil service rules by executive order. And when they did so, they weren't constrained by the Administrative Procedures Act (APA), which typically requires notice-and-comment periods and other hurdles to implement federal regulation. The Supreme Court said as much in *Franklin v. Massachusetts* and *Collins v. Yellen.* This makes sense. The APA was designed to protect the governed from the constitutional overreach of federal agencies, not federal employees from their employer.

With this authority in hand, the next president could implement any number of "rules governing the competitive service" that would effectively curtail the administrative state. He could relocate agencies out of Washington, D.C.—a move that would decentralize the District of Columbia as the seat of power, revitalize overlooked small towns and cities, and move federal agencies closer to the communities they supposedly serve. It would also result in mass departures, as many D.C.-based civil servants would be unwilling to relocate—which would have the added convenience of avoiding severance costs for voluntary departures.

The president can also impose term limits, ensuring that no bureaucrat can serve a term longer than the president himself. This too is yet another hiring policy—a prerogative that ultimately belongs to the president pursuant to his ability to "prescribe rules governing the competitive service" (5 U.S.C. 3302). The appointed czar could lay the groundwork, so long as the president is ready to sign on the dotted line.

The final step to truly taming the administrative state is to actually *shut down* agencies that shouldn't exist. I made strong policy arguments during my own presidential campaign of why agencies—ranging from the Department of Education to the Bureau of Alcohol, Tobacco, Firearms and Explosives (ATF) to the Food and Nutrition Service (FNS) to the Federal Bureau of Investigation (FBI)—should probably be shut down entirely. The purpose here isn't to adjudicate the merits of abolishing each of these agencies (that could be its own separate book, and maybe it should be). My point here is just that a willing president has the toolkit to do it.

What would it look like for Americans to *actually* govern ourselves? For the people we elect to be the ones who actually make the laws? The federal government would be smaller, for one. *Much* smaller. It would be more responsive to the people. And it would leave more room for states to govern, to make laws tailored to the needs of their own citizens. Businesses would also be freed from the anchor of bureaucracy, red tape, and regulations that have been holding them back. Innovation would surge. So would our economy. People would prosper. Our Founding Fathers weren't afraid to think big and dream bigger. Two hundred and fifty years later, we shouldn't be either.

FIVE TRUTHS

1. The people we elect to run the government are no longer the ones who actually run the government: most legally binding edicts are issued by unelected bureaucrats, not elected representatives.
2. Three-letter government agencies write rules that constrain the behaviors of Americans, even though Congress never expressly authorized these agencies to write most of those rules—which the U.S. Supreme Court recently curbed in *West Virginia v. EPA*, arguably one of the most important Supreme Court outcomes of the twenty-first century.
3. Federal agencies like the SEC not only draft and enforce regulations but also adjudicate disputes through in-house judges, defying the separation-of-powers principle enshrined in the U.S. Constitution, a practice the Supreme Court just ruled was illegal.
4. The shift of power away from Congress and toward bureaucrats reflects a reversion to the monarchical worldview of old-world Europe, which was fundamentally skeptical of self-governance and democracy.
5. Correcting the overgrowth of the administrative state cannot be accomplished incrementally; it will require large-scale firings and shutdowns of existing agencies.

6

THE NUCLEAR FAMILY IS THE GREATEST FORM OF GOVERNANCE KNOWN TO MANKIND

"Yes, I grew up in privilege. Not economic privilege, but the ultimate privilege of having two parents in the home—a mother and a father—instilling in us a focus on education and a belief in God."

The first time I said it, I was giving a snide reply to an irksome college student who challenged me on my opposition to affirmative action by accusing me of having "privilege."

On its face, the idea that I grew up in "privilege" was laughable. My parents weren't poor, but they weren't rich. They came to America with little to their name. My mother had gone to medical school on a scholarship in India, but had trouble finding a job as a foreign medical graduate and so joined a last-minute residency opening shortly before giving birth to me. My father faced down unforgiving layoffs at the General Electric plant, eventually attending night school to become an attorney, all while working his day job in order to provide for our family.

So when a young college student who for all I knew probably had his liberal arts degree paid for by wealthy parents challenged me not on the merits but on *my* privilege, I responded instinctively.

"You and I both share a concern about inequality in America," I said with the intent of disarming him. "But here's the difference: *you* want to address racial inequality with racial quotas. I want to fix the root cause of that inequality—broken families that set up many kids for a disadvantage in life long before they ever enter kindergarten."

To his credit, the young man didn't strike back but really seemed to at least consider the argument.

So did I.

The more I considered it, the more I dug into the hard facts and statistics and trend lines and research, the more I spoke with the experts on this issue, the more certain I became. Growing up in a nuclear family is the ultimate privilege. And one that is under direct attack.

TALK LEFT, WALK RIGHT

When University of Virginia professor Brad Wilcox begins his sociology-of-family class, he makes things personal.[1]

"Is it morally wrong to have a baby outside of marriage?" he asks his students in an anonymous online poll. About two-thirds say no. But ask them if they "personally plan to finish [their] education, work full-time, marry and then have children," 97 percent say yes.

And when asked "If you came home at Thanksgiving and told your parents that you (or your girlfriend) were having a baby, would your parents freak out?" that number jumps to 99 percent.

The disconnect is not limited to UVA.

The most educated Californians (those with at least a college degree) are the most likely to endorse family diversity (85 percent), and the least likely to have children outside of marriage themselves (just 20 percent of college-educated California parents are unmarried).[2] Another survey found that among college-educated liberals ages 18 to 55, just 30 percent were willing to agree that "children are better off if they have married parents," yet 69 percent of such parents were married themselves.[3]

Today the progressive elite are "talking left, walking right," when it comes to the nuclear family. They know that raising children in a traditional family structure—with two married biological or adoptive parents—is better for the kids and adults alike. Overwhelmingly, this is what they choose for their own family. Yet they are unwilling to "preach what they practice" when it comes to public policy.[4] They've learned the secrets to success, but they are unwilling to share it with those who could use it the most. And children—especially the ones who are already the most disadvantaged—are paying the price.

Raising children in stable, two-family homes shouldn't be a luxury good reserved for the elite. It is the ultimate privilege, and one that should be widely shared.

A NUCLEAR BREAKDOWN

I hate to start out with a bunch of statistics, but the numbers don't lie: Objectively speaking, the nuclear family is rapidly becoming an endangered species. In 1960, 73 percent of children lived with two parents in their first marriage.[5] By 2014, just 46 percent did. The decline comes as childbearing has been decoupled from marriage. In 1960, just 5 percent of births happened outside marriage. In 2021, that figure jumped to 41 percent; for black babies it is 70 percent.[6]

As a result, children in the U.S. have the highest rates of living in a single-parent household in the entire world.[7] The demographic shift is real. So is the cultural one. As Johns Hopkins University sociologist Andrew Cherlin has explained, starting in the late 1800s, traditional American sources of identity like family, religion, and community began to be replaced with an emphasis on happiness and personal growth.[8] Historian Steven Mintz of the University of Texas has observed similar trends, noting that in the U.S., values like "interdependence and filial duty" have been supplanted by weakened kin ties, potentially accelerated by high rates of mobility and dispersion. Being part of a family just isn't what it used to be.

This shouldn't come as a surprise. Today's culture not only accepts, but celebrates, the destruction of the American family. *Modern Family* has replaced *Leave It to Beaver* in defining what today's family unit "should" look like. Marriage is an oppressive institution driven by the patriarchy; its goal is purely to "disempower women and keep old hierarchies intact."[9] Divorce, the *New York Times* explains, is now an "act of radical self-love."[10]

It's not just marriage. Going "no contact" with aging parents is a feat of courage; abandoning elderly relatives over non-politically-correct views is praised for drawing healthy boundaries to separate oneself from those with toxic views.[11] "Childless by choice" is not merely a choice, but an identity marker, the kind of slogan you can proudly slap on a bumper sticker or cropped tee.

But the stakes unquestionably get higher once children are involved. "Family diversity"—which Brad Wilcox defines as "the idea that all family forms are equally valid and valuable for kids"—is considered "a mark of moral progress in society."[12] Every family is unique and special, whether that means children raised by single parents, or stepparents, or grandparents, or blended families, or anything in between. Some definitions go ever further: the concept of "chosen family" has recently gone mainstream.[13] *Blue's Clues* and *Teen Vogue* promote the ideology, to show children that family is what you make of it, and that biological and adoptive ties mean nothing.[14]

We live in an age of radical individualism, where we want for nothing, not even one another.

Activists have taken up the call. NGOs like Family Equality now preach that "[t]here is a myriad of unique ways" to become parents, and that "[n]one is preferable to the other"; Black Lives Matter advocates for "disrupting the Western-prescribed nuclear family structure" itself.[15] The traditional family unit is now taboo. The notion is antiquated, backwards. Its proponents are bigots, anti-choice, trying to impose their own ethical and religious beliefs on the freedom-loving crowd. Killing the free-spirited buzz, if you will.

But is family breakdown really a good thing? Does the ritual incantation of "diversity" and "acceptance" mean that we must blind ourselves to the advantages that come with having two loving parents in a stable home?

Of course not. So let's discuss these advantages with both eyes open.

CHILDREN THRIVE IN MARRIED, TWO-PARENT HOMES

Common sense suggests that children do best when raised by both parents, who are married to one another. So does the evidence.

Ben Carson has written a whole book on it, called *A More Perfect Union*. The figures are dire. Children in fatherless homes are four times more likely to experience poverty, suffer from obesity, become pregnant as a teen, or drop out of high school. Indeed, 71 percent of high school dropouts and 85 percent of children with behavioral disorders are from fatherless homes. Absent fathers increase the likelihood of drug use, theft, attacks, and arrests.

But of all the figures I've seen, this one stood out: a child who grows up without two married parents is more likely to wind up in jail than get a college degree. For children raised within a nuclear family, the outcomes are reversed: they are three times more likely to get a college degree than ever see the inside of a prison cell.

In virtually every area of life, having two married parents helps kids succeed, even in surprising ways. Like the NBA. When most of us conjure up an image of an NBA player, we think of someone like LeBron James, an unquestionably gifted player born to a sixteen-year-old mother in a rough neighborhood in Akron, Ohio, who fought his way out of poverty to the NBA. But he's an outlier. According to an analysis by the *New York Times*, between 1960 and 1990, nearly half of blacks in the United States were born to unwed parents.[16] But during this same period, approximately twice as many black NBA players were born to married parents compared to unmarried parents. The result? "[F]or every LeBron James, there was a Michael Jordan, born to a middle-class, two-parent family in Brooklyn, and a Chris Paul, the second son of middle-class parents in Lewisville, N.C., who joined Mr. Paul on an episode of 'Family Feud' in 2011."

This shouldn't be a surprise. With two parents, there is, on average, twice as many resources—love, time, money, attention—to go around. There's another person nearby when a little girl falls off her bike, to read to a child at night, to pick up an infant when he cries. From the parent's perspective, there's someone else to shoulder some of the burden, emotionally and financially, not just every other weekend, but all the time.

Of course, none of this is to say that every child raised in a two-parent family will do better than every kid who is not. Hardship often selects for greatness, but that doesn't mean we should create hardships for the next generation. President Franklin Delano Roosevelt may have never had the fortitude to be the leader who led the U.S. to victory in World War II if he hadn't faced adversity as a younger man when he contracted polio and lost the ability to use his legs. Would the U.S. have lost the war if FDR had never had polio? Would the eastern half of the United States be occupied by the Nazis and the western half by the Japanese? It's not crazy to wonder. But that's still a far cry from saying that we want more people to contract polio.

There are plenty of successful people who were raised by a single mother—Barack Obama, Jeff Bezos, Oprah Winfrey, and Eminem among them—but that doesn't negate the fact that, empirically, kids raised in two-family homes are much more likely to succeed.[17] Obviously, some, even many, children are able to defy the odds. But the odds are still against them.

Indeed, some of the biggest *proponents* of two-parent families are those who were raised by single moms and struggling grandparents—people who most acutely, and personally, felt the loss. And they are derided for speaking the truth. Obama, for example, was accused of "parroting . . . weaponized myths"[18] for acknowledging that "too many fathers are MIA, too many fathers are AWOL, missing from too many lives from too many homes."[19] My friend and former classmate (and also President Trump's vice presidential nominee) Senator J. D. Vance was raised by a drug-addled mother, a carousel of men, and, eventually, his Mamaw; he knows, better than most, that this is not an ideal scenario. Yet Vance has been criticized for making the bold claim that "if you actually raise kids in stable families, they're much more likely to be prosperous, and I think that's what we all want, really, is kids to grow up in healthy, happy situations."[20] Progressives, it seems, are willing to discount not only the empirical evidence, but the lived experience of those who have overcome such odds.

Other people may look at the numbers and question cause and effect. Rich people are more likely to get married (true) and they are more likely to have successful kids (also true), so maybe all this talk about "marriage" is really just a convoluted way to say that rich kids tend to do well. But Melissa Kearney, an economist at the University of Maryland and author of *The Two-Parent Privilege*, has considered this possibility. As it turns out, the benefit of growing up in a two-parent family holds even when comparing families in the same income bracket. Poor kids from two-parent families do better than poor kids from single-parent homes; middle-class kids from two-parent families do better than middle-class kids whose parents are divorced, and so on. "These benefits do not simply reflect the fact that richer people tend to marry at higher rates," she explains.[21] "Children of married parents generally have better outcomes even when controlling for the age, race, and education level of the mother."

Others, like Harvard sociologist Christina Cross, argue that "access to resources, more than family structure," matters for determining success, particularly for black children.[22] Perhaps the numbers reflect that more people are cohabitating, living in loving, stable, committed two-parent households, but remaining unmarried. And maybe cohabitation is just as good for kids.

But none of that is true. Preliminarily, cohabitation isn't what's driving the unmarried-parent crisis. According to U.S. census figures, only 8 percent of kids are living with a biological parent and that parent's partner.[23] But even that number overstates the number of kids living with cohabiting parents, since it includes partners who are not the child's other parent. Most kids who live without married parents in the home are doing so because their parents were never married, and do not currently live together (if they ever did).

Further, cohabiting parents are much more likely to split than those that are married. In fact, two-thirds of cohabiting parents will split before a child is twelve; just a quarter of married parents will do so.[24] Cohabitation simply doesn't offer the same stability as marriage.

Others may similarly argue that divorce is not necessarily bad for kids, so long as the father stays involved. And a father's involvement postdivorce does help. There's no question about that. But it doesn't entirely make up for the loss of a second parent in the home. Children of divorce still earn less, have lower educational achievement, and have more psychological problems than their married-parent peers.[25] "The way I think about [it]," Kearney explains, "is if kids who live with two parents through their whole childhood have sustained access to the resources of two parents, and kids whose parents were never married are more likely to have missed out on all of the parental resources from the second parent, kids of divorce are somewhere in the middle."[26]

But what about abusive marriages? Don't those harm kids? Isn't divorce a better outcome for them? No doubt, but the fact that not every marriage lives up to the ideal of a perfect, happy, nuclear family doesn't mean that we should abandon the ideal. Conservative writer Jonah Goldberg makes the following analogy: There are a lot of teachers who molest kids, but we don't abandon schools as an institution.[27] The same is true of abusive spouses. They should be imprisoned. They should be forced to stay far, far away from their ex-wives and children. But the existence of abusive men does not require the abandonment of marriage as an institution.

To the contrary, studies show that children are much more likely to be sexually, physically, or emotionally abused by a cohabiting boyfriend or stepparent than a married, biological dad.[28] About eleven times more frequently. So, to lower the overall instances of abuse in our society, we should be maintaining as many parental unions as possible.

Here's another truth I can let you in on: the traditional family isn't just good for the kids. It's good for the adults too. As Wilcox has shown, "today, most marriages are happy, the odds of getting divorced are now well below 50 percent, and married parents (ages 18 to 55) are happier than any other comparable group."[29] The narrative that marriage is about women being hidden away in the kitchen and that parenting is hell on earth is the kind of doom-and-gloom messaging that is not only counterproductive to raising happy kids, but also refreshingly wrong.

THE NUCLEAR FAMILY IS THE HEART OF SOCIETY

The decline of nuclear families isn't just bad for the individuals involved, but for society as a whole.

As Aristotle explained two thousand years ago, the family and state are deeply intertwined. The state, he believed, was like the body, and families were like organs of which it was composed. If you kill the body, the individual hand or foot cannot live. The state, then, was necessary for the functioning of the family.

The opposite is true as well. A body cannot live without a functioning heart and lungs; it cannot live up to its full greatness without feet and hands and elbows and ears. That's why Pope Leo XIII wrote that "the domestic household is antecedent, as well in idea as in fact, to the gathering of men into a community." The family is the first unit of community, the first time an individual is socialized into a particular group.

Before a child is citizen or a voter, he is a member of a family first.

Which leads to the sociological understanding of the familial role in relation to the state, which is often a functional one. The purpose of a family is to transmit culture to children, to teach them. A parent scolds a child for lying so that he learns that lying is morally unacceptable; a child is put in time-out so that he learns that taking something from someone else is wrong. We get most of our religion and ethics at home. And our language. Our values. We learn not just from what our parents tell us, but from the examples they set. From what they do, and what they don't do. Children are born barbarians—a fact I must remind myself of when my four-year-old announces he has space boogers and insists on munching the invaders—and it is our job as parents to civilize them.

That is why strong families lead to strong states. Families are the lynchpin of society. This isn't just a cliché. It's true. As former secretary of education William Bennett has written, "the family is the first form of community and government"; it is "the first, best and original Department of Health, Education and Welfare."[30] Strong families provide the foundation for strong civic institutions, strong churches, strong communities, and ultimately, strong cities, strong states, and strong nations.

That is precisely why, as Goldberg explains, "progressives of all labels have had their eye on the family."[31] It is the state's biggest competition. Devaluing the role of family was a core strategy of communism too. As George Weigel wrote in his biography of Pope John Paul II, the "hardest-fought battle between [the Roman Catholic] Church and [Poland's communist] regime involved family life, for the communists understood that men and women secure in the love of their families were a danger."[32] To address this threat, the state set housing, work schedules, and school hours "to separate parents from their children as frequently as possible." Apartments were built small so that "children would be regarded as a problem." Children were forced to start school at 6 or 7 a.m. so they almost never saw their parents; others were sent away to schools removed from where they lived. Communists understood that, for their ideology to take hold, they needed to get to the children first.

I suppose one way to think about it is this: if you value personal freedoms, pluralism, strong civic engagement, and small government, promoting the nuclear family is a must; if you value state-imposed, top-down views of right and wrong as decided by the progressive elite, then a strong nuclear family is an obstacle to be overcome.

Now, do I believe that most progressives are consciously trying to destroy the nuclear family so that they can assert unmediated influence on our nation's youth? Probably not. But it's hard to deny that progressives are trying to exert more and more control over our children's minds—through state-sponsored pre-K, less school choice, drag queen story time at libraries, critical race theory in public schools, and an almost complete progressive takeover of academia—and that, objectively, weakening the nuclear family makes that indoctrination a whole lot easier.

Politics and philosophy aside, the empirical evidence shows that strong families lead to societal benefits beyond those that accrete to individuals alone. Studies show that states that have higher levels of marriage, and particularly higher levels of married-parent families, also have more economic growth, less child poverty, and far less violent crime.[33] The effect is not small: studies show that "the share of parents who are married in a state is a better predictor of that state's economic health than the racial composition and educational attainment of the state's residents."[34] Impressive stuff.

Less crime. More economic growth. Happier citizens. More successful kids. Less progressive brainwashing. All good things. But is there a way to help make it happen?

HOPE IS NOT LOST

Conventional wisdom holds that even if the downfall of the nuclear family is a lamentable fact, there's not much we can do about it. Even some conservatives, including *New York Times* columnist David Brooks, share this view: "We've left behind the nuclear-family paradigm of 1955.[35] For most people it's not coming back." We can't force people to marry; we aren't going to outlaw divorce. If we want to help disadvantaged kids, we should just focus on improving schools and widening the safety net.

That thinking is as simplistic as it is irresponsible.

There are plenty of things we can do to incentivize and encourage marriage. At a minimum, we can repeal all the taxpayer money used to disincentivize marriage. A "do no harm" policy, as Jonah Goldberg has described it.[36]

There is unquestionably harm that needs undoing. An unintended side effect of welfare policies designed to help single mothers—from President Lyndon Johnson's misleadingly named "Great Society" project—is that many single mothers stand to make more money by being married to Uncle Sam than to the father of their children.

And the evidence suggests people respond to those incentives.

Take the very black community that Johnson's policies were designed to purportedly help. In the 1950s, prior to the passage of the Great Society, the black fatherlessness rate was 9 percent. Today, after decades of policies that incentivize family breakdown rather than family formation, that number is close to 45 percent.[37] Black Americans are not meaningfully better off economically today than they were prior to even the civil rights movement—a damning indictment of the government's attempt to play a productive role rather than a destructive one for broad segments of the population they set out to "help."

We could also consider evaluating our existing policies through the lens of supporting family formation.

Hungary is the rare example of a country that has been able to put family-focused policy into action, and has been reaping the rewards. Under Viktor Orbán's leadership since 2010, the government announced major policy reforms to promote births by married couples, including generous tax deductions, down payments for homes, and exempting women with at least four kids from income tax for life. We're not talking a measly $3,000 tax credit here. When adjusted for Hungarians' average annual incomes and cost of living, the Institute for Family Studies has estimated that the housing benefit alone would be the equivalent of up to $250,000 for a family with at least three kids.[38]

And that's not even mentioning the other incentives. One of the most creative is what they call the "baby-expecting loan."[39] Contrary to how it sounds, it's not for pregnant women. It's a wedding gift, available to any woman who is under forty when she gets married. The loan is worth the American equivalent of about $75,000, and can be taken out as soon as you're hitched. When you have your first kid, the interest stops accruing. After the second kid, 30 percent is written off. After the third, you don't have to pay back the loan at all. If you're not married, you can't take part. But the initiative is quite popular: in the six months after the program launched, Hungarian banks issued more baby-expecting loans than housing loans.

The results have been astounding. Marriages more than doubled.[40] Births are up too. The age-adjusted fertility rate is up from 1.23 in 2010 to around 1.59 in 2021.[41] There were other effects as well. Abortion rates were cut in half.[42] And according to a prosecutor general's report, the number of registered crimes fell from 447,186 to 165,648 from 2010 to 2019.[43]

The Hungarian model is almost surely not the right answer for the U.S., but understanding it may open our minds to solutions we haven't thought of yet. At a minimum, it provides a strong counterpoint to those who throw up their hands, claiming that changing marriage and birth rates can't be done.

Fortunately, there's another example of successful family policy that is much closer to home: the military. The U.S. military boasts a strong pro-marriage culture. And its policies reflect it.[44] Married enlistees get more cash via a housing allowance; cohabiting enlistees are treated as single. Married partners are also eligible for health benefits that unmarried partners do not enjoy. Spouses, and spouses alone, are eligible for relocation assistance when a service member is deployed overseas.[45] If your wife wants to go with you while stationed in Germany, the government will help her get a visa, a job, move her belongings, and more; if you're just playing house, you get nothing.

But it's more than the cash, of course. It's the whole culture. Studies show that people are 75 percent more likely to get divorced if they have a close friend who is divorced, and 147 percent more likely to get divorced if they have several divorced friends.[46] The opposite is also true. When most of the people around you are married, you're more likely to get married too. There's a social effect, where marriages beget more marriages. It becomes normalized, expected even.

The result is that the military enjoys, in the words of two scholars, "marriage rates [that] bear an anachronistic resemblance to those of the 1950s era."[47] Members of the military marry young, and at high rates. And perhaps most strikingly, there are no racial disparities.[48] For civilians, researchers consistently find that race is one of the biggest predictors of marriage, even after controlling for education, employment, and childhood family structure; in the military, there is no racial divide.

Perhaps that's why, when asked what he would do if he could enact "one policy to encourage marriage or help the people who are in marriage," Wilcox didn't hesitate: "I think there are lessons we can learn from the U.S. military that could help us understand how to advance both structural and cultural assistance to families, to make marriage more appealing and more accessible to ordinary Americans."[49]

THE LIBERTARIAN CASE FOR FAMILY POLICY

Much of this chapter so far has focused on the *conservative* case for the family unit: every *actual* "great society" throughout human history required a strong family institution in order to flourish as a nation. The family grounds our identity as individuals. And individuals, both children and adults, thrive when they live within the structure of a nuclear family.

Strong industrial policy types who favor state power to promote conservative values tend to favor the adoption of affirmative profamily policies in the United States. If the family is inherently good—indeed *required*—as an organizing unit of a well-functioning nation, then why shouldn't the nation use its resources to help promote more of that good?

Libertarians find these traditional arguments anathema—not because libertarians are antifamily, but because they are anti-state. The libertarian view on the matter goes something like this: The reason the nuclear family is the organizing unit of a flourishing *nation* is that the nuclear family fosters flourishing *individuals*. So if it's in the best interest of an individual to be part of a nuclear family unit, then all else being equal, consenting adults will organize themselves and raise their kids accordingly—without any nudge from the government to do so. Sure, some fathers (or mothers) will abscond, leaving their kids to grow up in a suboptimal environment that, at statistical scale, will cause rates of crime, poverty, and homelessness to be incrementally higher than they might otherwise be. But the peril of state intervention to try to engineer that outcome is far greater—so the libertarian argument goes.

Yet there's a separate *libertarian* case for the nuclear family itself. It's not just that experiencing the love of your family first opens your heart to the love of God (the Christian conservative view). Nor is it just that the family serves as an organizing unit that bolsters the proper functioning of the polity (the Aristotelian or "New Right" view). It's that a prevalent, well-functioning nuclear family obviates the need for an expansive welfare state—the archenemy of every libertarian.

There is a pragmatic component to the libertarian case. Strong families mean less crime. That means less jail—which is the ultimate restriction of freedom by the state. Strong families also mean less poverty, which means less welfare, less Medicaid, less people on the government dole. That means lower taxes. And less government involvement in people's lives overall. I'm not the first to make this connection. Almost twenty years ago, Rick Santorum said that being profamily means being pro–limited government: when you have strong families, "the requirements of government are less."[50] Of course they are.

There's also a more philosophical case to be made. Being profamily means creating policies that recenter the primary seat of governance—for raising children, for choosing where and how to live, for setting and adhering to values—away from the state and toward the family. It is, almost by definition, the rare use of state power designed to minimize the role of the state. From this vantage point, the goals of the profamily movement and libertarians are once again aligned.

As a libertarian-nationalist conservative myself, I find the arguments for profamily federal policy far more persuasive than, say, for industrial policy. In the latter case, the government collects and showers taxpayer money onto favored industries over disfavored ones. Yet which industry (or company) is favored versus disfavored is determined by which ones most effectively lobby the decision-makers in Congress and the administrative state. That's inefficient at best, and corrupt at worst. Leave the allocation of capital to the market, not the government.

By contrast, profamily policies that directly reward family formation and preservation are not naturally fertile ground for special-interest lobbying—unless the "special interest group" is the set of Americans who are part of stable families or aspire to become part of one. And if *that* counts as a special interest group, I'm not too bothered by it.

But at least as things stand today, the question for policymakers isn't whether to promote families or let the free market decide. It's a question of whether to come to the defense of families, or allow our current government policies to continue to dismantle them. Jonah Goldberg likens the situation to William F. Buckley Jr.'s line about moral equivalence: "If one man pushes old ladies in front of oncoming buses and another man pushes old ladies out of the way of oncoming buses, you simply cannot describe both men as the sort who push old ladies around."[51] If one party wants to use government power to destroy families, and the other wants to use government power to protect them, the two uses of government power are hardly the same.

In my life, I've reaped the blessings of the traditional family twice over. First, by having two loving parents, who instilled in me the importance of family and education and hard work. And now, having a beautiful, smart, funny wife by my side, and two children we call our own. I wake up every morning to my family. My wife beside me, and my sons just down the hall. We eat breakfast. We play silly games. We learn together. Heck, we traveled all ninety-nine counties in Iowa in a bus together—twice. How many families can say that? But I couldn't imagine my life any other way.

We know the keys to success. To happiness. To prosperity. We've known them for years. The "success sequence": Complete school. Get a job. Get married. Have kids. In that order.

Now it's time to share the secret, far and wide. To fling open the doors of opportunity not just for the children of California's educated elites, but for the children of Chicago's South Side and rural West Virginia. I'll shout these truths from the pages of this book, so that you can whisper them into your child's ears. That way the next generation won't be burdened by the discomfort of those who would rather spread misinformation that makes children suffer than share the truths that help them succeed. So that when you tuck your child into bed tonight, you know you've imparted one more life lesson, and a crucial one at that.

FIVE TRUTHS

1. Children raised in stable two-parent families are statistically more likely to succeed in education, avoid poverty, and stay out of jail compared to those raised in single-parent homes—not by a little bit, but by a *lot*.

2. Strong families create strong nations, reducing the need for an expansive welfare state and government intervention in personal lives. States with higher marriage rates see more economic growth, less child poverty, and lower crime rates: a state's share of married parents is a better predictor of economic health than race or education levels.

3. Lyndon Johnson's misnamed "Great Society" project was supposed to help black families, but its effects have been catastrophic for them—by creating the incentives for family breakdown.

4. Profamily policies in Hungary to incentivize marriage and family stability have resulted in lower crime rates, higher economic growth, increased birth rates, and improvements in happiness—proving that change is possible.

5. The first and easiest profamily policy that U.S. policymakers should adopt is to eliminate government-manufactured *disincentives* for family formation—by rolling back the disastrous precepts of LBJ's "Great Society."

7

REVERSE RACISM IS RACISM

I was in second grade in Evendale, Ohio, when I watched Dr. King's "I Have a Dream" speech for the first time. It was 1992. My teacher rolled a dusty TV into the classroom on a cart. As kids, we were always excited to "watch TV" in school, but this time was different. Dr. King dreamed that his four children would grow up in a country where they would be judged not on the color of their skin, but on the content of their character.

The moment stuck with me. Dr. King spoke not just of *his* dream, but a dream that all Americans could share. It was my father's dream, which brought him to this country to build a successful career at the local GE plant. It was my mother's dream, which allowed her to become a geriatric psychiatrist treating Alzheimer's patients in Ohio nursing homes. And it was my dream too—the one that allowed me to go in a single generation from being the middle-class kid of Indian immigrants to becoming the founder of multiple multibillion-dollar companies and a candidate for the president of the United States.

In America, there are no castes. There is no aristocracy. Every person is born equal. Both in the eyes of the law and in the eyes of the overwhelming majority of good, decent American people.

That's the American Dream.

The idea that someone would look at their skin color and predict something about the content of their character—the content of their *beliefs*—was abhorrent to Dr. King. The purpose of the civil rights movement was to defeat a cultural and legal tyranny of the *majority* that restricted what racial minorities were permitted to do, permitted to *achieve* in America.

Today, however, it is somehow racist to acknowledge that King meant what he said. To take his words at face value. To share in a vision of America that is color-blind, not in the literal sense, but when it comes to how we treat one another.

In June 2023, Professor Kevin Kruse of Princeton University mocked people for using Dr. King's quote to celebrate the end of race-based affirmative action, referring to it mockingly as "The Only Martin Luther King Jr. Quote They Know." A journalist for the *Guardian* wrote, "the man upon whom [conservatives] will heap their performative praise with social media virtue-signaling is MLK, a caricature of a man whose likeness has been made palatable for white consumption.[1] Like BLM, CRT and USA, the people whom King fought against have now managed to flatten a three-dimensional symbol to a three-letter, chant-worthy phrase worthy of demonization or deification."

To people like this, it is even more racist to acknowledge how far we've come in accomplishing that dream. It is racist to acknowledge that things are not perfect, of course, and that there are a tiny minority of truly hateful, racist people, or to acknowledge that most Americans today are not racist.

But these things are true, and worth saying.

BEYOND THE PROMISED LAND

Safeguarding against a tyranny of the majority was a central concern of our Framers. As James Madison wrote in Federalist No. 51, "It is of great importance in a republic not only to guard the society against the oppression of its rulers, but to guard one part of the society against the injustice of the other part. Different interests necessarily exist in different classes of citizens. If a majority be united by a common interest, the rights of the minority will be insecure."

The original Constitution ratified in 1789 addressed such concerns imperfectly, which the authors of the Reconstruction Amendments aimed to rectify. "No State shall . . . deny to any person within its jurisdiction the equal protection of the laws," the Fourteenth Amendment reads. But a significant gap remained: *states* were required to treat people equally, but private businesses were not. That's why, nearly a century later, civil rights activists fought to codify additional protections in federal law itself to prevent private-sector discrimination—and they succeeded. "I've seen the Promised Land. I may not get there with you. But I want you to know tonight, that we, as a people, will get to the Promised Land," Dr. King foretold in Memphis, Tennessee, on April 3, 1968, the night before his murder.

And eventually, we got there. That's controversial to say, but it's the truth. Yes, there's a ritual incantation I could recite about the myriad historical inequalities that black Americans have faced, but that's not the point I'm making right now. I grew up in the 1990s, in a nation where citizens could cast their ballots freely without limitations on race or gender; where it was unthinkable that a hotel or restaurant—or for that matter, a hospital or university—would deny service based on someone's skin color. Dr. King's promised land was one where little white boys and little black boys could play together without regard to their race or creed. I know we got to that promised land because it's where I grew up: The two neighbors to the left of our house were white; the two neighbors to our right were black. We all played together without giving our skin color a second thought.

To say that things are vastly better now than they used to be should not be controversial. It should be obvious.

Yet here we are.

At almost precisely the moment when we reached the promised land that MLK envisioned, when the train began pulling into the station, so to speak, ensuring equality for all under the law, a new generation of so-called "civil rights activists" rejected it outright.

The intellectual fountainhead of this new generation is Ibram X. Kendi, whose website bio described him as "one of the world's foremost historians and leading antiracist scholars." "The remedy to past discrimination is present discrimination," he argues. "The remedy to present discrimination is future discrimination." I believe this encourages, rather than fights, racism. It reduces individuals to racial groups, to be divided into the oppressor and oppressed. It is a dream in which children are judged on the color of their skin, as compared to an ever-shifting racial hierarchy constructed and reconstructed in the name of equity, never complete. For this, Kendi was awarded a coveted MacArthur "genius grant" for his work and handed the keys to a new antiracist research center at Boston University.

In less than a century, civil rights activists who fought for race neutrality had been effaced and outright replaced by a new wave of progressive activists who fought for a new form of racial discrimination. When we finally moved beyond the kind of invidious racism that stopped Rosa Parks from being able to sit in the front of a bus in Montgomery, Alabama, the claims about racism in America became more histrionic than ever—about a racism that was so invisible that they had to label it "systemic."

There's something especially peculiar about this. One can imagine a world where civil rights advocates successfully enshrined race-neutral policies into law and yet invidious racial discrimination nonetheless got worse. Where, in the decades following the Civil Rights Act, even more restaurants and hotels denied service to black people, where fewer black people were able to vote. Perhaps the law's opponents would have found loopholes, or the cultural backlash would have proven so strong that local officials were willing to turn a blind eye to rampant discrimination.

Against that backdrop, Kendi's argument that we need more aggressive "antiracist" policies might be more persuasive.

But that's not what happened. At all. Over the next half century there was a remarkable *decline* in racism across America. Before the Civil Rights Act, there was a very real possibility that black Americans in the South could be turned away from a business on account of their race. Today it's unimaginable. I haven't met a single person who's even heard of something like that happening—at least not any time this century. Chances are, neither have you.

When the biggest civil rights battle of our day is to rename schools with "racist" namesakes like Dianne Feinstein and Abraham Lincoln, the war has been won.[2] When overt racism has been so completely eradicated that the only bias left is "implicit," the war has been won.[3] When companies are rewriting "blacklist" to "blocklist" in backend software code that no one will ever see, to combat psychological aggressions so small they are "micro," the war has been won.[4]

Yet it's in the face of *that new reality* that the next generation of self-proclaimed civil rights activists nonetheless switched to calling for racial discrimination of a new kind. Douglas Murray put it aptly in his sagacious 2021 book, *The Madness of Crowds*: "At the very moment when the issue of race might at long last have been put to rest, they have decided once again to make it the most important issue of all."

The new-wave discrimination is illegal, and it is wrong.

RACIAL DISCRIMINATION IS ILLEGAL

First things first: racial discrimination is illegal. It is illegal because the Constitution and the Civil Rights Act say it is.

The Equal Protection Clause was written in the wake of the Civil War to establish the equal legal status of the newly freed slaves. It was not written to give advantages to one racial group over another; it was written to *reject* them. "Our Constitution is color-blind," Justice John Harlan wrote in his famous *Plessy v. Ferguson* dissent in 1896. "[It] neither knows nor tolerates classes among its citizens."

Opponents of the color-blind view argue that the Equal Protection Clause permits the government to discriminate on the basis of race in order to achieve more equal racial outcomes. To make this claim, they argue that the Equal Protection Clause could not have been intended to ban government action that would *help* black people because the same Congress that passed the clause also created the Freedman's Bureau. The Freedman's Bureau, the argument goes, was one of the boldest legal programs designed to help the newly freed black people, and offered benefits exclusively to blacks.

But as legal academics have persuasively explained, the Freedman's Bureau afforded benefits to the recently freed *slaves*, not blacks writ large.[5] And its goal was decidedly not to ensure equitable outcomes in the vein of the modern antiracism movement today. As Justice Clarence Thomas has explained, the legislative history of the Freedmen's Bureau Act makes clear that "the equality sought by the law was not one in which all men shall be 'six feet high'; rather, it strove to ensure that freedmen enjoy 'equal rights before the law' such that 'each man shall have the right to pursue in his own way life, liberty, and happiness.'" The goal was equality, not equity.[6] There is nothing in the text of the Equal Protection Clause, or the historical record, that suggests otherwise.

Racial discrimination is also outlawed by the Civil Rights Act.

Now, there are plenty of laws in our thick U.S. Code that are ambiguous and hard to understand. But the Civil Rights Act is not one of them. Title II, which applies to restaurants, hotels, and other businesses that serve the public, states that "all persons shall be entitled to full and equal enjoyment of goods, services [and] facilities . . . without discrimination on the ground of race, color, religion or national origin."[7] Pretty clear. Title VII, which governs employment, is arguably even clearer: "It shall be an unlawful employment practice for an employer to . . . discriminate against any individual . . . because of such individual's race, color, religion, sex or national origin." Easy.

Certainly, our lawmakers could have added "unless such discrimination is intended to help a member of a historically oppressed group," or "unless the victim of such discrimination is a member of the oppressor race," but they didn't. In truth, they probably couldn't have, because that kind of language would violate the Equal Protection Clause, but that's kind of the point, isn't it?

But even if we understand that our laws, as currently written, do not allow the kind of race-conscious reallocation of resources the antiracists demand, it is still worth asking what the law *should be*. Laws, and even the Constitution, are just words on paper. They can be changed. So if we were starting from a blank slate, what should we do? Should we, as a society, condone or promote discrimination against certain races as a means to achieving racial equity?

No. We should not. For many reasons.

ANTIRACIST POLICIES ARE RACIST

First, these policies are racist. And—I can't believe I have to write this— racism is bad. It sows resentment and division, and reduces individuals to racial stereotypes. And really, it's just unfair.

To state the obvious: many of these "antiracist" policies are nakedly racist against whites and Asian Americans.

The most prominent example is affirmative action in higher education. High-achieving Asian Americans are told they need to give up their spots at America's elite institutions to make way for black and Hispanic kids. Or worse, that they suffer a personality defect that no amount of hard work will ever be able to overcome.

Affirmative action's supporters claim it helps poor, disadvantaged black kids, but it doesn't. Most beneficiaries of affirmative action at Harvard, Princeton, and Yale come from high-income families.[8] Many are rich kids from Nigeria and Kenya.[9] Besides, if you want to help the poor kids, why not just help poor kids? Why just the black ones?

Supporters are also fond of claiming it's a "thumb on the scale," a tiebreaker when two candidates have nearly equal qualifications.[10] It's not "really" discrimination if it's just a fudge factor, they claim. That's bogus. The benefit of being black is enormous. Obviously! Or the schools wouldn't need to consider it! But let's talk numbers. Blacks get, on average, a 230-point boost on the SATs.[11] That means a white applicant with a 1500 score or an Asian applicant with a 1550 is evaluated the same way as a black student with a 1270.[12] As a result, an Asian applicant at Harvard who scores in the top academic quintile has about a 10 percent chance of being admitted. It's very unlikely he'll get in. But a black applicant? There's a 55 percent chance he'll be given the golden ticket.

It's true that the Supreme Court has, at long last, banned the practice. In *Students for Fair Admissions v. Harvard*, the Supreme Court held that Harvard's practice of penalizing Asian American students violated the Civil Rights Act. And when the University of North Carolina did it, the discrimination violated the Equal Protection Clause too.

But that doesn't mean affirmative action is going away. Already, schools are scheming on how to prevent too many Asian Americans from gaining admission.[13] Students are scrambling to rewrite college essays to revolve around their ethnic hardships or traveling back to Africa or Mexico to visit ancestors—wink, wink—since they can no longer check a racial box.[14] Even legislators are working to find under-the-radar ways to restore the quota system in America's colleges.[15]

And, of course, college admissions are not the only place where the antiracists have reared their ugly heads. Employment is just as bad. "You Can't Fire Only the White Guys," read one *Wall Street Journal* headline, detailing the case of David Duvall, a white man who claims he was fired to make room for his black replacement.[16] His company—like hundreds of others—had set a target to increase minority representation. And executives were financially incentivized to do so. It was a bounty scheme, paid out when white men were put on the chopping block. Those handed pink slips are supposed to just understand. The company wanted more "flair."

Or consider reparations. It used to be the kind of cockamamie idea that could be easily dismissed, but sincere, serious efforts are now underway. San Francisco convened an official commission. Their recommendation?[17] Five million dollars per black adult, the elimination of personal debt, guaranteed income of $97,000 a year for 250 years, and homes in San Francisco for one dollar per family.

The San Francisco proposal hasn't gone anywhere yet, but in some places, race-based cash transfers are already happening. Ask Tyler Lynn, a high school Spanish teacher for more than twenty years. In Oregon, where he works, teachers have to renew their licenses every few years. There's a $192 fee. But only if you're white. If you're black, or a member of another statutorily defined racial minority, you can apply for reimbursement. Lynn's skin color isn't dark enough. So he won't get the $192 refund check in the mail.

This goes all the way up to the federal level. As of this writing, the Biden administration has just approved a plan that pledges more than $5 billion to black farmers, explicitly implementing racial discrimination. Even NPR was recently forced to admit that the "equity goals" of this program were "sloppy."[18]

The private sector's in on it too. Virtually every major company has pledged to discriminate, although they would never call it that explicitly. McDonald's has pledged at least $3.5 billion a year that it will give out to nonwhite business vendors; Starbucks has pledged $1.5 billion a year; Disney, $1 billion.[19] And then they brag about it, as though this specific kind of racism is a hallmark of virtue.

Education, jobs, money. Three things that Americans find relatively important. But in "life, liberty and the pursuit of happiness," life comes first. And here, again, we see racism parading as antiracism. Even when the allocation is a matter of life or death.

I'm talking about Covid drugs. The kind that used to be in extremely short supply. When the FDA first authorized them for emergency use, there wasn't enough to go around.[20] So the FDA authorized them only for "high-risk" patients—and racial minorities.

As a result, New York made scarce medicines available to all racial minorities regardless of age or underlying conditions. Minnesota devised an "ethical framework" that prioritized black eighteen-year-olds over white sixty-four-year-olds—despite the fact that the latter are at vastly higher risk.

When the program was exposed, the FDA immediately dismantled it and apologized. I'm just kidding. The agency defended it, claiming "there are no limitations on the authorizations that would restrict their use in individuals based on race." No limitations? None? It's too bad the Constitution isn't written on the back of a pill bottle.

In a warped way, it makes some sense: logically, one way to close the racial gap in morbidity rates is to kill more white people. But I never thought anyone would really do it. A willingness to kill Great-Aunt Esther, so that young Camden can recover a week more quickly. For "equity."

It shouldn't be hard to see why this kind of race-based thinking would be upsetting, especially to the races for whom the antidote is perpetually out of reach.

VICTIMHOOD ISN'T BLACK-AND-WHITE

Antiracists sometimes argue that this racial favoritism is morally righteous because black people were uniquely and more gravely discriminated against in the past. Favoritism now is merely balancing the scales of justice. Ta-Nehisi Coates implicitly makes this case in his well-known 2014 article in the *Atlantic*, "The Case for Reparations," in which he details the exquisite pain of black people in America to argue that the moral ledger between blacks and whites is not yet square.[21]

Such a claim is spurious. Preliminarily, as Columbia University linguist John McWhorter explains in his essay "Against Reparations," "for almost forty years America has been granting blacks what any outside observer would rightly call reparations."[22] It should be noted that he wrote that in 2001—well before the latest wave of race-based handouts. Our welfare system began in the 1930s to help widows; by the 1960s it had expanded to "help" black people, in large part due to "claims by progressive whites that the requirements of the new automation economy made it unfair to expect blacks to make their way up the economic ladder." Today there are myriad government programs available solely to black people, and solely on account of their race. Some of them allocate billions.

But more broadly, blacks are not uniquely situated as far as historical discrimination is concerned. Throughout our nation's history—indeed, all of human history—we have often treated each other poorly, sometimes on account of race. The black experience is hardly unique. Even in America.

Japanese Americans faced internment during World War II. Jewish Americans have often been discriminated against, as have other racial minorities. To this day, Native Americans experience harsh treatment in our legal system, which has not yet adapted to the complexities of life in tribes.

Even slavery itself wasn't black-and-white. Prior to the eighteenth century, the practice was uncontroversial and widespread. And it wasn't a racial phenomenon. As Stanford University professor Thomas Sowell has explained, "People of every race and color were enslaved—and enslaved others.[23] White people were still being bought and sold as slaves in the Ottoman Empire, decades after American blacks were freed." Even in America, there were black slave masters, and there were white slaves.[24] Slavery was and has always been driven by human greed, not racial animus.

I say this not to minimize slavery, but to contextualize it. Every racial group in American history has been a target of racist attacks. Every single one. And members of every group have done the attacking. And if that's true, the intellectual edifice of "oppressor" versus "oppressed" paradigm disintegrates. Accordingly, using prior victimhood status as a justification for reallocating resources is not only morally repugnant, but intellectually unsound.

"TO HELP OR TO HURT"

Legal and moral quandaries aside, there would still be an argument to be made for such policies if they at least served to help black people, to dispel hateful stereotypes, to spur their achievement, to make their lives better in some way.

But the truth is that antiracist policies do precisely the opposite.

First off, antiracism reinforces negative racial stereotypes. This shouldn't be surprising, since fixating on racial stereotypes is one of progressive orthodoxy's founding principles. The National Museum of African American History and Culture in Washington, D.C., has a whole article on "whiteness" where it ascribes traits like "objective, rational linear thinking," "delayed gratification," and punctuality as emblems of white culture.[25] What does that suggest about blacks?

The exhibit may seem trivial, but the messaging runs deeper. Antiracism seeks a revolutionary change in how America works, based on what McWhorter calls "the faulty assumption that black Americans are the world's first group who can only excel under ideal conditions."[26] It is a dogma that says that blacks are incapable of thriving in the world as it is today, that they are victims, and helpless ones at that.

Let's do an experiment. Look at these two stories that are, or could be, taught as part of a school curriculum. Which of these two do you think is official education policy, and which is an outcry against the system?

A. "A long time ago, way before you were born, a group of white people made up an idea called race. They sorted people by skin color and said that white people were better, smarter, prettier, and that they deserve more than everybody else. Racism is the unfair rules they make about race so that white people get more power, and get treated better, than everybody else."

B. "I am the direct descendant of the North American slave trade. I am not oppressed. I am not a victim. There's the truth about slavery and racism, and also the truth that we ended slavery. We had two consecutive Black secretaries of state, we had two consecutive Black attorneys general, we have Black billionaires, Black mayors. I live inside of my skin and I don't walk around in an oppressed [sic] country."[27]

A., unsurprisingly, is excerpted from a book included in New York City's new critical race theory curriculum.[28] And B. is a black parent railing against that type of indoctrination.[29] Which of these two narratives, do you think, sets black children up for success? Which one makes black children feel motivated and proud? Which one sounds like racist gibberish?

Then there's a related phenomenon, the soft bigotry of low expectations. It tells black and Hispanic children that when they are unable to meet a bar—whether it's a standardized test or being punctual or getting a math question right—the problem is the bar, and it will either be eliminated for everyone or lowered for them alone. They are deprived of the encouragement needed to keep trying, of the incentive to persevere, and the thrill of success achieved on equal terms.

But let's get more concrete. Lowering admissions scores for blacks and Hispanics has resulted in them being admitted to colleges for which they are academically underprepared; as a result, they drop out at much higher rates.[30] We know this because of a natural experiment that occurred when California banned affirmative action in 1996. Ending the double standard led to a 55 percent increase in the number of black and Hispanic students who graduated in four years, and a 51 percent increase in the number that majored in STEM (science, technology, engineering, and mathematics) fields.

Defunding the police has led to even more dire consequences. In the aftermath of the movement, murders skyrocketed, and disproportionately so in the black community. In 2019, about 7,500 black Americans were murdered; in 2020, it was nearly 10,000.[31] That's more blood on the anti-racists' hands.

In fairness, it wasn't black people who were calling to defund the police. The vast majority of black Americans—around 81 percent—wanted the same or more officers on the street.[32] That's not surprising if you have even a basic understanding of what it's like to live in a community plagued by violence. Which a lot of black people do. As Harvard law professor Randall Kennedy has found, "[o]ne out of every twenty-one black men can expect to be murdered, a death rate double that of American servicemen in World War II."[33] Of course they want more police. They don't want those police to be kneeling on their necks, fair enough, but they also don't want them replaced by peace-sign-wielding-nonviolent-hippies-with-degrees-in-intersectional-gender-studies gently urging murderers to do less murdering through art therapy.

Simply abolishing police, and crime along with it, is the kind of magical thinking of people who live in the warm comfort of their suburban cocoons. In other words, it was a policy pushed by the mostly white, educated progressive elites. It was virtue-signaling masquerading as progress, and it left the "oppressed" to pay the price.

Anyone who said this at the time, of course, was derided as a racist. But now that we've seen the terrible consequences of the "defund the police" movement, it has slowly become permissible in liberal circles to admit that the whole thing was an absolute failure. Every time Joe Biden tells us that the answer to our problems is to "fund the police," as he did during his most recent State of the Union address, he should be reminded of the damage his party wrought during the "summer of love."

He should be reminded that words, and policies, have consequences.

SACRIFICING TRUTH AND HAPPINESS ON THE ALTAR OF JUSTICE

Antiracist policies cause a lot of harm. To specific groups—the whites and Asians who are supposed to shoulder the burdens of such policies with a smile, the blacks and Hispanics whom it is supposed to help—sure, but also to our society as a whole. And they do so in at least two related but distinct ways.

First, the nonstop focus on race is unhealthy. There are various ways I could make the case—skyrocketing anxiety and depression among the woke, increased polarization and sense of societal disconnect—but most people just feel it.[34] The incessant negativity. The us-versus-them mentality. The race wars. It's a bad *vibe*.

Earlier this year, a court ruled that Zack De Piero, a Penn State professor, could sue his employer for creating a hostile work environment.[35] He was forced to undergo bias trainings, to watch videos and participate in a "breathing exercise" so that Penn State's white faculty could experience what George Floyd felt; white and nonblack people of color were instructed to "hold their breath just a little longer—to feel the pain." When he objected, the university told him "there is a problem with the white race" and insisted that he just needed more training until the lessons stuck. He sued. The university claimed it was doing all this to *combat* racism, but the court didn't buy it. "When employers talk about race—any race—with a constant drumbeat of essentialist, deterministic, and negative language, they risk liability under federal law."

That's a win for De Piero, but what does it mean for the rest of us? The "constant drumbeat of essentialist, deterministic, and negative language" is everywhere. NFL stars kneel during the national anthem. Outdoor clothier The North Face offers a 20 percent off coupon for taking a course explaining that systemic racism is why black people don't hike. Starbucks launches a #racetogether campaign so that office workers and baristas can solve race relations via a quick chat while picking up coffee on their morning commute. We're told that roads are racist.[36] Birds are racist. Math is racist. Voting, of course, is super racist. Everything is a problem, and it's all racism's fault. If Penn State's ubiquitous racial programming created a hostile work environment for De Piero, then the antiracist movement's ubiquitous racial programming is creating a hostile *world* for all of us.

This race essentialism is everywhere. There is no way to turn it off.

Second, the tactics of the antiracist movement are fundamentally illiberal. It is cultlike, promoting a strict orthodoxy that brooks no dissent. You are antiracist, or you are racist, there is no in-between.[37] And, as such, it impedes the search for truth.

McWhorter describes these tactics as the tenants of a "flawed new religion."[38] What it demands is not logic, but blind faith. If you operate in the world of reason, you cannot sing Harvard's praises for explicitly preferring black scholars in the academic job market but then shriek in horror at any suggestion that Claudine Gay, who resigned as president in 2024, was hired because she is black. That would be a contradiction. But if it is a religious belief, then the logical inconsistency is no barrier.

Worst of all, you're not allowed to point out these discrepancies. Dissenters are excommunicated, and scientists most of all. Take Roland Fryer, the black Harvard economics professor who found that police officers were 23.8 percent *less* likely to shoot at blacks than they were to shoot at whites.[39] When he first saw the results, he couldn't believe it himself. So he hired eight new staff members and redid the study. The results held.

But when he published them, the death threats rolled in. His reward for "following the science" was being forced to go diaper shopping for his seven-day-old daughter with an armed guard.

"The way to stop discriminating on the basis of race is to stop discriminating on the basis of race," Chief Justice John Roberts famously wrote in *Parents Involved*. True enough. But I would offer a corollary: "The way to stop making everything about race is to stop making everything about race." We are a nation of many people who define ourselves, as individuals, in many ways—men, women, socialists, conservatives, artists, accountants, mothers, uncles, gamers, chess players, bakers, first-generation college students, union pipefitters, people who like to dress up as furry animals and attend conventions, etc.—and this is a source of our strength. We are a pluralistic nation built on a promise of equality, indivisibility, liberty, and justice for all. It's time we start acting like it. Only then will we get back to the promised land.

FIVE TRUTHS

1. The modern race activists' claim that "the only remedy to past discrimination is present discrimination" directly flouts the legal prohibitions in the Civil Rights Act and the Equal Protection Clause of the Fourteenth Amendment.
2. By institutionalizing antiwhite and anti-Asian racism, affirmative action also fosters a greater degree of anti-black and anti-Hispanic racism: there's no better way to get someone to become a racist than to take something away from them on the basis of their own skin color.
3. The social cost of accusing someone to be racist is low, while the social cost of being labeled as racist is high—creating a new culture of fear that has suppressed open debate about racialized policies.
4. It's not a coincidence that it is precisely as the U.S. has approached, or even *reached*, the "promised land" that Martin Luther King Jr.

envisioned that race activists have become more strident in their claims about systemic racism.

5. Color-blind merit is foundational to the American way of life—the fact that our Founding Fathers fell short of respecting that ideal because of the existence of slavery should not be a basis for us to repeat their mistakes in the name of correcting them.

8

NATIONALISM ISN'T A BAD WORD

"I agreed with many, many things you said during—in fact, probably more than most other candidates—when you were running for president, but I still would not have voted for you, because you're an Indian."

That's how Ann Coulter opened the conversation the first time I spoke to her, several months after my presidential campaign had ended, during an episode of my newly relaunched podcast. I had invited her as a guest because I had seen her make a number of similar remarks about me during the presidential campaign, so I wanted to have a conversation with her about it face-to-face.

The press criticized her comment as racist, but that missed the mark. Ann Coulter's problem with voting for me *wasn't* my genetics or my skin color. Suppose I had been born to the exact same parents, at the exact same time, in the exact same place (Good Samaritan Hospital in Cincinnati), but I had been legally adopted at birth by fifth-generation white Americans . . . or even fifth-generation *black* Americans. Coulter says she would have had no problem voting for me.

"I've said it a million times. I think immigrants can wait a few generations before telling us what to do. I'm only talking about president," she told Dan Abrams of NewsNation.[1] "It's not racist. Blacks have been here longer than most whites. It has nothing to do with race. It has to do with being a citizen for at least three generations. I think that's a good rule."

I have my doubts about whether Ann Coulter is *actually* more ready to vote for the great-grandson of a Jamaican immigrant than she is for the grandson of an Anglo-Saxon British lord. But for the sake of discussion, let's take her at her word. The more interesting question at stake is two competing visions of U.S. citizenship.

U.S. CITIZENSHIP: CATEGORICAL OR SCALAR?

I adopt a categorical, cut-and-dried view of U.S. citizenship: if you're an American citizen, then you're every bit as much of an American citizen as anybody else. Period. Your skin color doesn't matter. Your ethnic heritage doesn't matter. The number of generations that your ancestors have been in the United States doesn't matter. What matters is that you owe your *sole* civic allegiance to the United States of America, not another nation.

Ann Coulter's view of U.S. citizenship is different: citizenship *isn't* just a categorical attribute. Rather, citizenship is a *scalar* concept: there are different degrees of "how American" you can be. A kid of legal immigrants born in the United States is not, all else equal, as "American" as someone whose ancestors arrived two centuries ago.

The view is worth taking seriously because a lot more people share this view than are willing to admit it. Once you believe that American identity is scalar, there's no reason to limit it to the number of generations your ancestors have been here. Other factors could matter too, like the culture of the country your ancestors came *from*. The daughter of immigrants from England or Canada who speaks with an American accent, and likes pizza and apple pie while watching baseball, might be, all else being equal, "more American" than the son of immigrants from Japan or Pakistan whose parents don't speak English and who himself speaks with an accent, who likes to eat mofongo and curry while watching cricket.

Here's the problem with that view: Who gets to decide which attribute is "more" American? Even the hypothetical example is confounded by myriad factual problems: pizza came from Italy, apple pie wasn't created in America, baseball is more popular than cricket is in Japan, and cricket is more popular than baseball in England. That wasn't just a cute example to prove the point. I'll challenge you to come up with a clean-cut hypothetical that works. Turns out it's hard to do—because the premise of scalar citizenship is fundamentally flawed.

That's especially true in America because our national identity has *never* been based on ethnic heritage, or skin color, or accent, or even the number of generations that your ancestors have been here. When you try to reinvent a narrative of American identity based on those attributes, it doesn't cohere.

Rather, citizenship—in modern America as in ancient Rome—is really based on one attribute: *loyalty.* Do you owe your undivided loyalty to the United States of America or not? If yes, and if you've gone through the process of expressing that in a manner legally recognized by our country's naturalization process, then you're a citizen. And if not, then you're not. That's why the final step of the naturalization process for immigrants requires a civics test and an oath of loyalty to the United States of America.

That's why "dual citizenship" is an oxymoron. You can't owe allegiance to another country if you've sworn an exclusive oath of loyalty to the United States. If those two countries were at war, or even had conflicting interests, it would be impossible for you to tell your fellow citizens in either of those countries that you were as loyal to the nation as other citizens who *hadn't* pledged allegiance to another country. I think it's bizarre—and deeply problematic—that there are U.S. citizens *today* who can be conscripted to serve the military of a foreign nation—because they are also citizens of that other nation. It's even more bizarre that there are elected representatives who are simultaneously citizens of other nations, without the requirement to disclose that fact to their constituents—which is a big problem. That's part and parcel of my *categorical* view of citizenship.

But if you adopt a *scalar* view of citizenship, loyalty is just one of several factors that matter. And every factor is simply a matter of degree. Suppose an American-born person's grandparents came to the U.S. from Germany and he chooses to spend time in that other country, and later chooses to become a dual citizen of that other country. That means he can vote in their elections, serve in their military, and carry a passport of that nation and identify as a citizen of that nation when traveling abroad. Is that person "more or less" American than the American-born son of the Pakistani immigrant who likes to eat curry while watching cricket, but who swears an oath of loyalty solely to the United States of America and to no other nation? On my categorical view, the answer is clear: sole loyalty and legal recognition is all that matters. On the scalar view, the answer is entirely amorphous.

ETHNONATIONALISM VS. CIVIC NATIONALISM

This leads us to the topic of another forbidden N-word: *nationalism*. The word carries a negative connotation. But it needn't be that way. Nationalism is a powerful force that has shaped the world we live in for good.

Nationalism reflects the worldview that citizens should support the interests of their own nation above those of other nations. It's often accompanied by the view that one's own nation is inherently superior, at least in certain ways, to other nations. I call myself an American nationalist because I believe that the United States of America is the greatest country on earth and that the first and sole moral duty of U.S. leaders is to advance the interests of U.S. citizens.

But a lot hangs on the concept of *citizenship* that we just discussed. If you believe (as I do) that citizenship is exclusively about loyalty to your nation, then nationalism is a civic concept—not an ethnic or lineage-based one.

With the exception of Native Americans, every American is either an immigrant or the descendant of one. We don't have a state religion. We don't pledge fealty to a monarch. There is no national ethnicity. Not only is there an absence of a national religion, monarch, or ethnicity; our commitment to the *absence* of one is essential to our national identity.

American national identity is grounded in a set of *ideals* that united a diverse group of people 250 years ago. The idea that you get to speak your mind freely, as long as I get to in return; the idea that you get to practice your religion, without the government getting in the way; the idea that you get ahead in America based on hard work and merit rather than the station of your birth; the idea of self-governance over aristocracy.

If that is the basis of American national identity, then what does it mean to be an American *nationalist?* It means you believe in the *exceptionalism* of these ideals—that these ideals form the backbone of the greatest nation known to mankind, and that it's our responsibility to bequeath these ideals to posterity because if the United States of America doesn't do it, then no other nation will.

People forget that nationalism, as a concept, dates to antiquity.* Before it was corrupted by Hitler and Stalin, it was an enlightened, liberal ideal. In the classical era, it was a solution to the tribalism and infighting that plagued ancient civilizations and, in particular, ancient Greece. As Victor Davis Hanson of the Hoover Institution has explained, the word *nation* itself comes from the Latin word *natio*. Back then, nationalism was considered "a progressive idea that, unlike the Greek city-state where people of the same language, roughly the same traditions, and the same ethnic background were politically fragmented, in Italy they came up with a new concept of unification" as "a more equitable and successful way of solving

---

* I credit Professor Hanson for his scholarly research and thoughtful commentary on this topic, which have informed my own views of why restoring nationalism is paramount to America's future.

145

rivalries between different people." Ancient Rome, he reminds us, "was a multiracial society like our own." It had incorporated most of Western Europe and parts of Northern Europe, Africa, and the Middle East too. It needed a way to unite its people. Given its diversity, unification based on ethnic or religious homogeneity wasn't an option. And given its liberal ideals, use of force was also off the table.

But there was a third solution. One that could bring together people of different races, ethnicities, religions, into a single country. One that Hanson describes as "very rare." So rare, in fact, that no civilization since Rome has been able to pull it off. Except the United States.

That solution is *civic* nationalism. It's the ability to unite a group of people based on a common national story. Of the pilgrims, who set out for America in search of a better life, and the Native Americans who helped them survive in a foreign land. Of our Founding Fathers, who sought to build a nation on ideals. Of Martin Luther King Jr., who fought for equality for all Americans. Of the great works of Ernest Hemingway and John Steinbeck and Georgia O'Keeffe and Louis Armstrong. And everything in between. A story that belongs not to any one of us, or any faction of us, but to all of us. As Americans. The idea of American *citizenship* is about pledging your *sole* allegiance to that nation founded on those very ideals.

Just like ancient Rome, America *isn't* just a place. It's a vision of what that place can be, grounded in that set of ideals. To pledge allegiance to those ideals, you have to first know what those ideals are. For a nation founded on a set of ideals, knowing those ideals is a more fitting precondition for full citizenship than is the act of being born in a particular geography.

We live in a moment where nationalism can actually be a force for good in America—an important tool for reviving national unity over a national divorce. I don't just mean national pride, which means you believe that you live in a great country. I actually mean *nationalism* in its own right.

Nationalism is usually a bad word, because it's usually conflated with ethnonationalism, where a homogeneous majority takes action to create further homogeneity within a country. The national identity of most countries is tied to an ethnic heritage, or a religion, or allegiance to a monarch—and *nationalism* in that context refers to the creation of an emphatic commitment to advance *that* national identity.

This raises complicated concerns for minority rights and relations with other countries, especially when nationalism is combined with territorial ambition. World history is fraught with countless cases of ethnonationalism gone awry. When your national identity is tied to an ethnicity, the objective of advancing the interests of your nation becomes tantamount to advancing the interests of your *ethnic group*. That awakens tribal, evolutionarily hardwired instincts that eventually end in a familiar destination: violence. History confirms that account time and again.

Take, for example, Nazi Germany. In the 1930s and 1940s, Nazi Germany, under Adolf Hitler, pursued an aggressive form of ethnonationalism aimed at establishing a pure Aryan race. This led to the systematic persecution and extermination of Jews, Romani people, disabled individuals, and other minority groups. The Holocaust, which ensued, resulted in the murder of six million Jews and millions of others in concentration camps. This extreme form of nationalism didn't just lead to genocide; it ignited World War II, causing widespread destruction and loss of life, reminding us of the catastrophic consequences of such ideologies.

Similarly, in 1994, Rwanda experienced one of the most horrific instances of ethnonationalism. The Rwandan Genocide saw the Hutu majority government orchestrating the mass slaughter of the Tutsi minority, leading to the deaths of approximately 800,000 people in just one hundred days. This ethnic cleansing was driven by deep-seated hatred and the desire to establish ethnic dominance, resulting in unimaginable brutality and the decimation of communities.

These examples underscore why "nationalism" gets a bad rap—and understandably so. But that kind of nationalism has no place in America, since our national identity isn't tied to an ethnic heritage.

Yet it risks rearing its ugly head again with the scalar view of citizenship. If citizenship is a categorical concept, ethnicity and genetics play no role in defining your national identity. But if your genetic lineage governs "how American" you really are, then your identity as an American becomes inextricably linked to your genetic lineage—which replaces civic nationalism with ethnonationalism just like it would in most ordinary countries since the time of ancient Rome.

FORTIFYING CIVIC NATIONALISM THROUGH A NATIONAL CIVICS EXAM

If we accept, as I think we should, that we are a country built on nationalism, on American exceptionalism, and that it is our shared ideals and history, rather than our ethnicity or religion or even country of birth, that define and unite us as a country, then we ought to take stock from time to time of how we're doing on those fronts. Democracy is fragile, after all, and nationalism—at least the good kind—is more fragile still.

Unfortunately, it's bad news almost all the way down. Today American pride remains at a near-record low. According to one Gallup poll, 39 percent of Americans described themselves as extremely proud to be an American, compared to 70 percent in 2002.[2] Per a different survey, 95 percent of Americans believe that understanding how our government works is important for the nation's success, but just 45 percent of respondents thought the U.S. was performing well in promoting such civic literacy.[3] They weren't wrong. Study after study shows that Americans' basic civic knowledge is very low, and dropping. Less than one in four Americans could name freedom of religion as one of the rights protected by the First Amendment, down from 56 percent in 2021; less than half of Americans can name all three branches of government, also a substantial drop.[4]

One solution: require every high school senior to pass the same civics test—and take the same oath of loyalty—that every immigrant is required to take before becoming a full citizen, including gaining the right to vote. As a practical matter, we would start with the current generation; people who already have the right to vote would not have that right taken away.

The system is already in place for those born outside the United States. Prior to gaining citizenship, immigrants must clear two fundamental hurdles. One is to score 60 percent or higher on a ten-question civics exam, drawn from a pool of one hundred questions about U.S. history and government that one can study beforehand. Easier questions include naming the current president and explaining what the Declaration of Independence did (according to the government's cheat sheet, "declared our independence" is an acceptable answer). Harder questions include naming one of the Founding Fathers who wrote the Federalist Papers. You don't have to score perfectly, but you need to know a majority of what's in there—and rightly so. The second requirement is to pledge *allegiance* to the United States of America. After all, that's really what citizenship itself is about.

If we require these hurdles of immigrants, we should require them of people born within the United States as well. Not to punish our children, but to give them the gift of civic knowledge and of citizenship earned.

You would still enjoy core constitutional rights even if you fail these standards. Call those the "immunities" of citizenship. Just as the government can't seize the property of a green-card holder or prosecute him for a crime without due process, neither could the government do so to someone born in the U.S. who failed to take the loyalty oath or pass the civics test. But just as an immigrant doesn't get to enjoy the *privileges* of citizenship (such as the right to vote) until he passes a civics test, neither would the natural-born citizen.

This is the obvious consequence of a civic nationalist worldview. If citizenship is truly about loyalty to your country, there's no reason why we should apply more lax standards to certain Americans just because of the geographic location of their birth. Your genetic lineage or exact geographic location of birth is less important than whether you espouse the ideals of the U.S.

It's worth noting that this standard isn't nearly as demanding as that required by other countries like Israel or South Korea, which require mandatory military service on pain of criminal punishment for all citizens. Passing a civics exam and taking an oath of loyalty is minimal by comparison, but it's still a substantive requirement for enjoying the full privileges of citizenship.

What about for individuals who are handicapped and can't take a civics exam? There are exemptions for handicapped individuals in the naturalization process too, but the rare existence of individuals who are unable to take a test isn't a strong basis for negating the requirement itself. The same exemption and alternative path to assess the loyalty of naturalized citizens can be used for natural-born ones as well. Here's one easy way to handle it: six months of service in a military or first-responder role would be sufficient as an alternative to passing the civics exam for anyone. This also addresses the objection that if someone serves and is willing to die for their country, they should be able to cast a vote in that country with no further questions asked.

There's also the question—a reasonable one—of whether the government could constitutionally restrict the right to vote to those who pass a civics test and take the loyalty oath. There's strong reason to believe that it could. For all of our national history, both men and women could be citizens. Yet prior to the passage of the Nineteenth Amendment in 1920, women did not enjoy the right to vote in all states. Minors are citizens. And they enjoy lots of constitutional rights. The Supreme Court has held they have the First Amendment right to engage in political protests at school (*Tinker v. Des Moines*) and the Fourteenth Amendment right to an equal education (*Brown v. Board of Education*). But they do not have the right to vote. Felons too are citizens of the United States, yet may be denied access to the ballot box (*Richardson v. Ramirez*). And in most states, those adjudicated to be mentally incompetent can be disenfranchised as well. Citizenship has never been coterminous with the right to vote.

There's one potential wrinkle in this argument: the Twenty-Sixth Amendment. That's the one that says that the right to vote cannot be denied or abridged on account of age. Recall that under my proposal, new eighteen-year-olds would have to meet these requirements, but existing voters would not. That could be a problem, but not an insurmountable one. The policy goal here has nothing to do with age and everything to do with increasing the civic commitments of all voters—so it could be implemented in a manner decoupled from age as well. Logistically speaking, there are three potential workarounds: (1) amend the Constitution (unlikely), (2) apply the test-and-oath requirement to everyone (less unlikely, but still unlikely), or (3) frame the legislation as applying to all new voters (so that it is tethered to registration status, rather than age), so as to remove any implied age-based condition altogether. But the practical concerns of this particular proposal aside, the fact remains that voting is a *privilege* of citizenship, rather than an inalienable *right*. And that means that the right to vote can be tied to responsible stewardship.

Voting is not unique in this respect. You could perform the same exercise on any range of other privileges. Does citizenship entitle you to, say, Social Security or particular medical benefits? Not quite. There are citizens who may be denied these entitlements, and conversely there are noncitizens who collect them.

So the exercise goes on, until we understand that asking "what you get" is the wrong question to ask about citizenship. It's not about what you get at all. It's about what you give. For men in South Korea, or for anyone of either gender in Israel, that means mandatory military service. In our country, it should mean knowing the minimum attributes of the ideals that define our nation—or at least living them out through some form of national service. That's the basic obligation that *every* citizen owes this nation. Voting isn't really an entitlement of citizenship; the obligation to vote as a loyal and knowledgeable American is a duty of citizenship, one that is critical to mend a fraying nation.

FORTIFYING CIVIC NATIONALISM BY DEMANDING LOYALTY FROM OUR ELECTED OFFICIALS

The thing that a citizen gives his nation is undivided *loyalty*. What the citizen rightly expects back in return from the leaders of his nation is their undivided loyalty back to him. When that trust is broken—when elected officials put their own personal interests or the interests of other nations ahead of those of the United States—our faith in the U.S. government and civic institutions erodes. For that reason, the first and sole duty of U.S. elected leaders is to U.S. citizens.

Yet that's a failure of U.S. leaders in both major political parties right now.

Today our congressional leadership is more concerned about protecting the territorial border between Ukraine and Russia than the one protecting the United States itself. As of this writing, the United States has authorized $175 billion in foreign aid to Ukraine alone since 2022.[5] That includes 10,000 javelin missiles, 31 tanks, and more than 1.5 million artillery rounds. These shipments make the United States the single largest military donor to Ukraine. For comparison, Germany has contributed less than half of what the U.S. has provided, France has contributed a paltry $700 million, and Spain even less than that—even though these countries face a greater geopolitical threat from Russian expansion than the United States does.

The United States' outsize military donations may not come as a surprise, but what many people don't realize is that the $175 billion our government has authorized also includes over $40 billion for *nondefense* spending. Over $25 billion has been earmarked for economic support for the Ukrainian government, businesses, and humanitarian programs. There's no doubt that war-torn Ukraine could use funds to bolster its domestic programs beyond warships and planes, but so could the United States.

The top priority of U.S. defense spending should be to protect the U.S. homeland itself, not economic programs abroad. It's no coincidence that after a two-decade period in which our nation has waged foreign wars in the Middle East that haven't advanced our own national interest, our homeland defenses are weaker than they've ever been.

Consider the possibility of an electromagnetic pulse attack (EMP) from a nuclear adversary. Should such an attack occur, the U.S. could be cast in darkness for over a year, sent, in an instant, to the era before the Industrial Revolution. The initial E1 pulse of an EMP would disable electronically controlled protective devices, while its subsequent E3 pulse would drive intense currents to physically damage transformers, which could lead to a complete collapse of our electrical grid. To counter this threat, we need to bolster our critical infrastructure now, by standardizing equipment, replacing Chinese-made transformers with domestic ones, building a stockpile of reserves, hardening existing infrastructure, and supporting the development of microgrids. None of this is cheap. Yet we throw billions at Ukraine.

Or cyberattacks. Our military, economy, business, and civilian infrastructure, from smartphones to traffic lights to fuel pipelines, all depend on secure internet access. Our adversaries know this and are constantly engaging in cyber espionage and probing for weaknesses. The risks are expanding exponentially, as is the potential fallout.

We are also more vulnerable to missile attacks than ever before. China and Russia both have hypersonic missiles that can travel twenty times the speed of sound, reaching anywhere on earth in under an hour. We don't. And we aren't prepared to deal with them. The missiles can stay low to the ground, and maneuver in flight, evading even our most advanced detection mechanisms. We need billions dedicated to shoring up these defense capabilities. Urgently.

Our national debt is arguably at its most precarious position in our national history, at $34 trillion and ballooning by the day. Yet we continue to expend foreign aid to other countries whose national debt per capita is less than ours. Elected leaders who owe an obligation to their own citizens must, at the very least, require zero-based budgeting for all foreign aid and investment in multilateral institutions, ranging from the World Health Organization to the United Nations, asking the primal question: How does this investment of U.S. dollars advance the interests of U.S. citizens?

Our elected officials must also avoid using their positions of power to enrich themselves. Most obviously, that means ending insider trading for members of Congress. It's indefensible. And widespread. In December 2022, Nancy Pelosi's husband sold 30,000 shares of Google just one month before the Department of Justice sued the tech giant for alleged antitrust violations.[6] In 2020, Senator Dianne Feinstein sold off millions of dollars of stock right before the coronavirus outbreak crashed the market.[7] These aren't isolated examples. A New York Times analysis found that ninety-seven member of Congress—ninety-seven!—[8] had bought or sold stock that intersected with their congressional work.

Other means of wallet-fattening abound, though such practices at least have the decency to shroud themselves in a modicum of secrecy. Foreigners and special-interest groups funnel dark money through super PACs and other entities to fund campaigns, not only corrupting officials but sowing distrust in the electoral process.[9] Sometimes the not-quite-bribery is more overt. Take the case of District of Columbia mayor Muriel Bowser. Her super PAC—set up to support her upcoming reelection as the then-sitting mayor—raked in hundreds of thousands of dollars. High-level donors were rewarded with an exclusive invite to join her on a trip to China.[10] But even smaller companies hoping to do business with the city felt the pressure: "If you want to continue to have good favor with the mayor, [donating to the super PAC] is something you do," one public contractor told the *Washington Post*.[11] Arguably a pay-to-play scheme, with extra steps. Such practices may not be technically illegal, but they are perhaps immoral, and a seeming breach of the sacred duties that elected officials owe to their constituents.

Then there are the lobbyists, incessantly calling on our elected officials to persuade them of the merits of their clients' positions through good old-fashioned advocacy—and the promise of a lucrative lobbying gig once the congressman leaves office. In 1970, less than 5 percent of legislators went to work for lobbying firms; now half of retiring senators and a third of house members do.[12] And when they leave, they're in for a big raise: a 1,400 percent increase, *on average*.[13] None of this helps American citizens. It doesn't even pretend to.

Perhaps most significantly, the promise of sole loyalty requires reining in the conflicts associated with dual citizenship itself. I argued earlier that "dual citizenship" is an oxymoron, but for as long as the concept is recognized by the U.S., we must at least impose a requirement that U.S. public officials abdicate any foreign citizenship they may hold. Today the scale of the problem is unknown: most bizarrely of all, there isn't even a public *disclosure* requirement of whether these public officials enjoy dual citizenship. A public official's sole loyalty should be to the citizen he serves. If that's not the case, the bare minimum requirement is for those political candidates to tell the voters as much before asking for their votes.

This isn't an unfamiliar notion in the law. When I ran for president, I completed a required financial disclosure questionnaire, which, when taken literally (as I did), required an inordinate level of effort, cost, and detail to provide. But I did so willingly and without complaint because

I understood the purpose—namely, so that the electorate could understand any *financial* conflicts of interest that might affect the policies that I would advance as a presidential candidate.

But if we go to this length for financial conflicts of interest, it's beyond puzzling that we don't require the same for the *ultimate* conflict of interest: a conflict of national loyalty itself.

The solutions are clear: End new foreign aid commitments to nations whose national debt per capita is less than ours. Stop funding multilateral institutions hostile to our own sovereignty and which don't advance our national interest. End insider trading for public officials, super PACs, and the revolving door of lobbyists who enrich legislators at the expense of their constituents. Require mandated disclosure of dual citizenship for our own public officials. Restore the idea that the sole obligation of U.S. public officials is to U.S. citizens. Only then can we repair the crumbling foundations of civic nationalism upon which our democracy is built.

FIVE TRUTHS

1. American national identity is rooted in civic ideals, not ethnicity. Ethnonationalism ties national identity to ethnicity, often leading to violence and division, but civic nationalism promotes unity and shared loyalty.
2. Nationalism needn't carry a negative connotation; it can unify diverse groups around shared ideals, as it did in ancient Rome and can in modern America.
3. Citizenship is about undivided loyalty to a nation. That's why dual citizenship is an oxymoron: you cannot pledge your loyalty to two different nations at the same time.
4. Every high school senior should be required to pass the same civics test and take the same loyalty oath to the United States, before

enjoying the full privileges of citizenship, for the exact reason we require immigrants to do the same before becoming citizens.

5. Loyalty is a two-way street: the first and sole moral obligation of leaders is to U.S. citizens. It's no coincidence that Americans feel less loyal to their country when U.S. elected leaders are less loyal to their own citizens.

9

FACTS ARE NOT CONSPIRACIES

By this point in the book, we've seen a familiar pattern. Something bad exists in the world; the left then uses that "bad thing" to deny the existence of something else that is *true*; and if you call them out for it, you risk being tarred with punitive labels. This has the effect of systematically stifling dissent. Over time, that results in the public acceptance of certain falsehoods over the truth.

The pattern is ubiquitous. It's a fact that there is a lot of suffering in the world; the nihilist left uses that fact as a basis to deny the existence of God. It's a fact that racism exists; the woke left uses it to deny the existence of equality of opportunity. It's a fact that a very small number of people suffer from a mental health condition called gender dysphoria; the sex-obsessed left uses it to deny that there are only two genders. It's a fact that global surface temperatures have tended to rise very slightly in recent years; the climate-obsessed left uses that to deny the value of fossil fuels. If you deny their narrative, they will label you a racist, a transphobe, or a climate denier.

This chapter deals with a different subject where I've observed the same pattern: the use of the label "conspiracy theorist" to sidestep confronting hard truths on subjects that most people find deeply uncomfortable. But in this case, it's not just the left who is at fault.

To be clear, pure *conspiracists* do exist—just as pure racists do too. Conspiracists are rabble-rousers who make baseless allegations with the goal of attracting attention by sowing public doubt. They're cynical, purely self-interested, or both. Take the allegation that the moon landing was fake. Sure, it's fair game to express any opinion in a free country, but there's no compelling shred of evidence *at all* to suggest the Apollo missions were artificially manufactured, or that the thousands of people who participated in them were telling a giant coordinated lie. It isn't credible. There's no factual basis to support it. It isn't a useful contribution to public discourse.

But the fact that there are some nut jobs out there can't be a basis to shut down legitimate challenges to the government or media as a "conspiracy theory," just as the existence of some malevolent racist somewhere can't be a basis to shut down legitimate challenges to the wisdom of affirmative action. Yet that's exactly what's happening today. Democrats and Republicans are both guilty of it. I've been on the receiving end of a lot of unfriendly labels in recent years—racist, transphobic, climate denier, Uncle Tom, you name it—but none was more damaging to my candidacy for president than the charge of being a conspiracy theorist.

My goal in this chapter *isn't* to vindicate myself on the specifics of any one debate where I sparred with the press or other candidates. It isn't even to relitigate the handful of supposed "conspiracy theories" that I reference in this chapter. Rather my goal here is to more deeply understand the modern tendency to dismiss likely explanations for uncomfortable facts as "conspiracy theories." It turns out the solution to this problem is the same as the solution to *every* problem we explore in this book. That gets to the heart of the most foundational premise of America's founding itself.

SAUDI INVOLVEMENT IN 9/11

Fourteen days before the first Republican presidential debate in Milwaukee, Wisconsin, I was interviewed by a podcaster Alex Stein. I had no idea who the guy was, other than the fact that he was supposedly an online comedian. With stilted humor, he asked me questions in rapid fire. Just after asking "if the moon landing was real," he asked me if I thought the attack on the United States on September 11, 2001, was an "inside job, or exactly as the government tells us."

I answered directly: "I don't believe the government has told us the truth. I'm driven by evidence and data. What I've seen in the last several years is we have to be skeptical of what the government does tell us. I haven't seen evidence to the contrary, but do I believe everything the government has told us about it? Absolutely not."

Apparently, that breached a third rail of American politics.

The *Wall Street Journal* had a field day roasting me for that response. The paper's editorial board, which had previously been respectful (even if not friendly) to my candidacy, published an extended piece titled "Vivek Ramaswamy Dives into Swamp Land," with the subheading "Did the presidential candidate really say that about 9/11?" Referring to the interviewer's question, they said "Mr. Ramaswamy should have run away from that one, if not right out the interview door." That was the heart of the criticism—not that something I said was false, but that it was in the category of the kind of question that ought not be asked in the first place.

The anaphylaxis was bipartisan. Democrat senator Chris Murphy from Connecticut tweeted: "If you want to be the GOP presidential nominee, you need to believe the government blew up the Twin Towers, and Osama bin Laden is an innocent man who's living under an alias in Miami." Former vice president Mike Pence said he was "deeply offended" that I didn't trust the 9/11 *Commission Report.* The *Wall Street Journal* went on to claim that the 9/11 Commission was "one of the better efforts at government accountability in recent memory," whose "findings have never been discredited by anyone credible."

But that's patently false—in fact, incontrovertibly so. The FBI declassified documents in recent years that reveal that the 9/11 Commission flatly lied about Saudi involvement in the attacks. The shocking details of just how wrong the commission was on this point were first reported extremely well by ProPublica, an outlet that does not typically stray too far outside the mainstream on issues like this one. The preponderance of evidence has become so great, in fact, that even the *Atlantic*—a publication I tussled with on the campaign trail on this very topic—has had to weigh in on it. In an article titled "New 9/11 Evidence Points to Deep Saudi Complicity," Daniel Benjamin and Steven Simon write that the official record of events presented in the 9/11 Commission's report "now appears wrong. And if our understanding of what transpired on 9/11 turns out to have been flawed, then the costly policies that the United States has pursued for the past quarter century have been rooted in a false premise. The global War on Terror was based on a mistake."

A key question confronted by the 9/11 Commission, then, was whether the Saudi government was involved in planning the attacks. The report concluded there was neither Saudi government nor royal family involvement. At the time, questions swirled around a forty-two-year-old graduate student who welcomed, housed, set up bank accounts, and gave rent money to the first two Al Qaeda hijackers after they landed in Los Angeles in January 2000—concerns that the FBI and 9/11 Commission flatly dismissed.

The Saudi student, Omar al-Bayoumi, claimed to have met the two terrorists entirely by chance. This was a laughable claim even at the time—that a forty-two-year-old graduate student randomly met two terrorists at the airport, and instantly befriended them to such an extent that he welcomed, housed, and *set up bank accounts for them*. Terrorist or not, I don't think any traveler to the United States has ever developed such an immediate friendship from a random encounter at a commercial airport.

Yet the 9/11 Commission report verified that Bayoumi's altruism was indeed in the name of hospitality as he claimed—dubious beyond all credibility. And FBI official Jacqueline Maguire testified to the 9/11 Commission in 2004 that Bayoumi's first meeting at a café with the hijackers appeared to be "a random encounter." To this day, Bayoumi maintains his innocence, and he has never been formally charged with a crime.

But the government had already collected evidence that Bayoumi's story wasn't all that it seemed. A 1998 FBI investigation revealed that rather than attend "graduate school" as he purported, Bayoumi frequented local mosques, doling out money for various causes and frequently and conspicuously videotaping visitors. The "graduate student" reportedly put up $400,000 to start a mosque in San Diego and all the while was paid a stipend and other expenses as a ghost employee of a Saudi contracting company, the FBI reported. Notwithstanding these facts, both the FBI and the 9/11 Commission emphatically supported Bayoumi's account of his relationship to the hijackers.

If you're hearing it for the first time now, it probably sounds like a bad joke. Anyone who believed Bayoumi's account of a "chance encounter" against the backdrop of these facts should be immediately fired from an investigative role in a police agency like the FBI. Yet if you publicly question that narrative, you are a tinfoil-hat-wearing conspiracy theorist, as if you were questioning the veracity of the moon landing. It's no different than, say, publicly opposing affirmative action in the summer of 2020, but being unable to have the debate on the merits because you were called a racist—except this time, Republicans and Democrats both would have shouted you down for questioning the narrative.

The "chance encounter" narrative was the official line for twenty years, but in recent years the FBI quietly changed its story. In documents declassified in 2022, the bureau affirmed that Bayoumi was in fact an agent of the Saudi intelligence service—who worked with Saudi religious officials and reported to the kingdom's powerful ambassador in Washington.

These revelations are now the focal point in a long-running federal lawsuit in New York, where 9/11 survivors and relatives of the 2,977 people who were killed are seeking to hold the Saudi government responsible for the attacks. Kudos to ProPublica for investigative reporting that the conservative press has chosen not to touch with a ten-foot pole. ProPublica is often viewed has having a left-leaning bias while the *Wall Street Journal* is right-leaning, but the facts at issue aren't partisan at all.

There are reasons to believe that successive U.S. administrations hid the Bayoumi revelations—not because 9/11 was an "inside job," but to provide public cover to the CIA for critical failures in the lead-up to 9/11. The two Saudis, Khalid al-Mihdhar and Nawaf al-Hazmi, were known to the CIA as Al Qaeda operatives. The CIA was watching as they joined an Al Qaeda planning meeting in Malaysia in early January 2000. But the agency reportedly lost track of the two when they flew on to Bangkok and then to Los Angeles on January 15. Embarrassingly, the CIA did not alert the FBI for more than a year after learning that the terrorists had entered the United States using their real names and Saudi passports.

Given the enduring mystery over how the CIA lost track of Hazmi and Mihdhar in Malaysia, former FBI investigators have speculated that Bayoumi might have been asked to approach the hijackers as part of a U.S. or Saudi intelligence operation to recruit them. At the time, former officials have said, the CIA was desperately trying to develop sources inside Al Qaeda.

The CIA has consistently denied that it allowed the hijackers to come into the United States as part of a failed recruitment effort. Former White House counterterrorism coordinator Richard Clarke cited this as a plausible explanation for the CIA's failure to track the first two hijackers and its abiding refusal to alert the FBI to their presence in the United States.

In light of this new reporting, it's worth revisiting the fact that in the frenzied days after the 9/11 attacks, when most flights were still grounded, dozens of well-connected Saudis, including relatives of Al Qaeda leader Osama bin Laden, were allowed to leave the United States on specially chartered flights.[1] According to a 2005 report from the *New York Times*, the FBI provided personal airport escorts to two prominent Saudi families, aiding their departure amid heightened security concerns.[2] When these facts first came to light in 2005, the bureau reacted with fury, insisting that their treatment of Saudi families did not indicate any preferential treatment for the Saudis. Anyone who suggested otherwise was treated as a conspiracy theorist.

Crucially, the reason these facts are collectively dismissed as a "conspiracy theory" in "swamp land" isn't that these data points are false. It's that they're *true*—which is what makes it so uncomfortable for establishment figures in both the media and government to confront. It's remarkable how quickly the *Wall Street Journal* editorial board maligned me for broaching the topic of government dishonesty about 9/11, *yet had absolutely nothing to say about the actual government lies themselves.*

This is the most paradigmatic case of how the term *conspiracy theory* is abused: use the term to bury a set of facts not because they are false, but because they are so patently and demonstrably true yet uncomfortable to acknowledge. Categorize an entire *topic* in the eyes of the general public as the sort of thing that only a crazy person would say. This allows the actors responsible for perpetrating the hoax to preserve their own credibility by not having to themselves make a claim that is falsifiable—but instead to create a pall of doubt on the entire discussion. Note that the *Journal* editorial board didn't criticize the facts I cited or the argument that I made, but just asked the broad sarcastic question of "whether the presidential candidate really just said that."

ORIGIN OF COVID-19

The tactic is now ubiquitous. Recall the public narrative around the origin of Covid-19 back in 2020. A global pandemic originated in China, specifically in the city of Wuhan. That city was home to one of the most sensitive biosecurity facilities in the world, known to conduct research on rare viruses. A pathogen with unique properties emerged from that very city in 2020. When international researchers tried to understand the source of the virus, the Chinese government stopped them from proceeding. Yet the account that the media and governments around the world publicly embraced was to say the virus resulted from animal-to-human contact in an open market, despite the fact that there was no documented case of an animal that had actually been infected with the virus.

You might have seen Jon Stewart, the former host of *The Daily Show*, raise this very issue during an appearance on *Late Night with Stephen Colbert*. Speaking in June 2021, Stewart launched into a bit about the origins of Covid-19 while his host looked on in nervous amazement.

"Oh my God," he said, "there's a novel respiratory coronavirus overtaking Wuhan, China. What do we do? Oh, you know who you could ask? The Wuhan novel respiratory coronavirus lab. The disease is the same name as the lab! That's just a little too weird, don't you think? Oh my God, there's been an outbreak of chocolatey goodness near Hershey, Pennsylvania; what do you think happened?"

This is what used to be called common sense. But when you use common sense too early, you risk being labeled a conspiracy theorist. That's why as soon as Stewart was finished, Stephen Colbert—who had recently performed a Broadway dance number with human-sized needles to celebrate the unveiling of a new Covid vaccine—asked him if he was working for Senator Ron Johnson, a Republican. The implication was clear: toe the line on the government's official narrative about Covid, which at that time relied on the much stranger (and much more racist, come to think of it) suggestion that the virus originated in a dirty wet market in Wuhan, right down the road from a coronavirus laboratory.

Speaking a couple of years after the incident, Stewart recounted some of the backlash he received from his liberal fan base.

"The larger problem with all of this," he said, "is the inability to discuss things that are within the realm of possibility without falling into absolutes and litmus-testing each other for our political allegiances as it arose from that. My bigger problem with that was I thought it was a pretty good bit that expressed kind of how I felt, and the two things that came out of it were I'm racist against Asian people, and how dare I align myself with the alt-right."[3]

The occasion for this speech, which occurred on Stewart's podcast, was a report from the Department of Energy that concluded that the virus likely originated from an unintentional lab leak in China. This was also mocked on the late-night circuit, with hosts incorrectly asserting that the Energy Department had no right to weigh in on the matter. (The department is, in fact, the group with the best capacity to investigate such things; it operates national laboratories that have advanced scientific and technological expertise, including in areas related to biosecurity and genetic analysis.)

This was part of a larger pattern to discredit anyone who asks questions. And it is a pattern that began right away, and right from the top. Before February 2020, for as Robert Moffit and Mary McCloskey have pointed out in a recent piece for the Heritage Foundation, several experts, including Dr. Kristen Andersen, raised the possibility that Covid seemed to have features that would suggest it was "engineered." Another expert also expressed doubts about a natural origin, pointing out the implausibility of the virus's specific mutations occurring in nature without human intervention. Yet, immediately after a pivotal conference on February 1, these same scientists publicly dismissed the lab-leak theory they had privately considered plausible.

Every day, new evidence points toward a lab leak as the most likely origin of Covid-19. A recent report in the *Times* of London found that "scientists in Wuhan working alongside the Chinese military were combining the world's most deadly coronaviruses to create a new mutant virus just as the pandemic began."[4] A report in the *Wall Street Journal* found that three researchers at the Wuhan Institute of Virology, including a U.S.-funded scientist, became ill in November 2019 with symptoms consistent with Covid-19, raising further suspicions about the lab-leak theory.[5]

More is surely on the way. It's only a matter of time before legacy publications sense that the tide is turning and begin reporting the facts as if they've known them all along, just like they are currently doing with Saudi involvement in 9/11.

This claim about the origin of Covid-19 was as laughable on its face in 2020 as it was in 2001 to claim that Omar al-Bayoumi was an overaged graduate student who randomly befriended three terrorists at Los Angeles International Airport and instantly came to love them so much that he helped them quickly obtain housing and bank accounts. In both cases, if you questioned either narrative, you were publicly exiled to the realm of "conspiracy theorist." Social media companies nearly universally censored anyone who claimed the Covid-19 virus leaked from a lab in China.

If 9/11 had occurred in the age of modern social media, there's little doubt that Facebook, Twitter, and YouTube would have done the same thing to those who alleged that Omar al-Bayoumi was a Saudi intelligence operative working with 9/11 terrorists as they did to those who said in 2020 that Covid-19 leaked from a lab.

TIMING IS EVERYTHING

There's a counterargument to consider: If these were truly malevolent high-level plots to dupe the public, then why would those same government actors *later* publicly disclose information that revealed their earlier lie? After all, it was the same U.S. government that lied about Bayoumi's Saudi ties that later declassified the documents proving that he was a Saudi intelligence agent. Similarly, it was the same U.S. government that denied that Covid-19 began in a lab in China that more recently admitted it was the likely origin of the pandemic. That wouldn't make sense if the government's goal were to mislead the public.

The answer to this conundrum goes back to my assessment of the motives of the deep state, back in chapter 5. It is easy to ascribe malevolence to bureaucratic actors, but that misses the mark. The truth is more frightening: they're doing it out of *benevolence* to the public. Generally, when the government hides the ball from the public, it's not some bureaucrat looking after his self-interest. It's some bureaucrat thinking he's looking after *your* best interests.

That explains why they went on to declassify the documents twenty years later. The real risk in the intervening period was that public knowledge of Saudi Arabia's potential involvement in 9/11 would unproductively sow chaos in Middle East policy. The U.S. needs to have a stable and productive relationship with Saudi Arabia to protects its interests and guard against even greater long-run threats in the region from Iran (or so goes the conventional wisdom, at least). The harm from the truth would almost certainly outweigh the benefits of geopolitical stability in the Middle East.

The same went for managing a global pandemic. If the public *knew* that the Covid-19 pandemic started in a lab in Wuhan, and further, that it was funded by the same U.S. taxpayer dollars and government actors who also funded research into the Covid-19 vaccines that were advanced via "Operation Warp Speed," then the public would have been more dubious to take those vaccines. On top of that, the diplomatic strain on U.S.-China relations wasn't worth it at a time when the people who led the U.S. felt that stability was more important.

But once that period of urgency had passed, it was "safe" to admit to the public what careful observers knew to be true. At the right *time*, it was deemed safe to publicly admit that a high-level Saudi intelligence operative in the U.S. had a direct role in working with and harboring multiple 9/11 attackers—because, frankly, the public doesn't care enough to let it disrupt our Middle East foreign policy goals. At the right *time*, it was deemed safe to publicly admit that Covid-19 *did* originate in a lab in China—because the policies viewed as necessary to contain the Covid-19 pandemic had already been implemented. And on top of that, U.S.-China relations deteriorated in the meantime for other reasons anyway.

Yet the irony of this approach is that it fosters more *conspiracism*. There's no evidence for the claim that 9/11 was an "inside job"—that U.S. government officials were involved in facilitating the attacks—but an otherwise ridiculous claim becomes more appealing once it becomes evident that the U.S. government definitively lied about another fundamental part of the attack. There's no evidence for the claim that the Chinese Communist Party *intentionally* created Covid-19 in a lab with the goal of releasing it and creating hell for the rest of the world—but when government actors around the world systematically suppressed the truth that it came from a Chinese lab at all, it is natural to ask the question of what else they're suppressing. This fuels rampant public distrust—and defeats the very "benevolent" intentions that motivated the noble lie in the first place.

This raises the question of which untouchable "conspiracy theories" *today* will be vindicated by government admissions twenty years from now. That's a question that most of our Founders would have asked if they were alive. Reviving our republic requires that alert citizens do the same.

If twenty years can change what we characterize as a "conspiracy theory" about 9/11, or if a mere two years can change what we characterize as a "conspiracy theory" about the origin of Covid-19—or countless other topics that we haven't discussed in these pages, from the Trump-Russia collusion mirage to the fact that the Jussie Smollett incident was staged—then it behooves us to at least be inquisitive about certain viewpoints that are vehemently dismissed as conspiracy theories today, but which are grounded in legitimate factual questions and may be thus vindicated in the future. Arguably no single topic tops that list more than getting to the bottom of the truth of what really happened on January 6, 2021.

FBI INVOLVEMENT IN JANUARY 6TH

In the great pantheon of "conspiracy theories," few today are as sensitive as those that dare to challenge the official narrative of the so-called January 6th "insurrection." While the public deserves the truth no matter how difficult, one can at least understand the sensitivities surrounding the jealously guarded 9/11 narrative. After all, 9/11 was the largest and most traumatic attack on American soil since Pearl Harbor, sixty years before. The 9/11 terrorist attacks claimed the lives of three thousand Americans and resulted in insurance losses of over $45 billion.[6] By contrast, four Americans died on January 6, 2021.[7] In terms of dollar damage, January 6th barely exceeds $1.5 million in damaged property, barely a rounding error next to the billion dollars in damage caused by BLM riots in the aftermath of George Floyd's death in 2020.[8]

Political leaders nonetheless continue to refer to January 6th in the most ominous and hyperbolic terms imaginable. Vice President Kamala Harris has compared January 6th to both 9/11 and Pearl Harbor.[9] President Biden has claimed January 6th was the worst attack on "our democracy" since the Civil War.[10] Even former president George W. Bush used the occasion of the twentieth anniversary of 9/11 to subtly suggest a comparison to January 6th.

As absurd as such comparisons are, they are unintentionally accurate in certain critical respects. Just as 9/11 served as a catalyst and pretext for the development of a vast national security apparatus to prosecute the War on Terror, so has the official version of the events of January 6th served as a pretext for the political weaponization of this national security apparatus against those who support President Trump. January 6th may be nearly three and a half years ago, but the notion that it was a Trump-inspired insurrection not only remains a key pillar of one of the major criminal cases against Trump, but is also the basis upon which states have attempted to remove his name from ballots.[11] Given everything riding on it, it's no wonder Democrats lash out at anyone who questions the official January 6th narrative.

The only problem is, even more so than 9/11, the official narrative just doesn't add up.

The first misconception about January 6th is that the FBI and other relevant authorities were simply caught flat-footed and had no way of knowing additional security might be warranted. FBI director Christopher Wray himself encouraged this misperception in an interesting exchange with Senator Amy Klobuchar, who asked Wray whether he ever lamented not being able to infiltrate the various groups to which January 6th was imputed so as to be in a position to prevent it.[12] Wray sheepishly sidestepped the question, never directly addressing FBI penetration of the militia groups in question. As it turns out, however, this penetration was more extensive than anyone imagined.

In September 2021, the *New York Times* begrudgingly acknowledged at least two FBI informants in the Proud Boys organization, confirming that one of them was texting his handlers in real time—*while in the Capitol*.[13] A subsequent report conceded there could be "as many as eight," and that "federal law enforcement had far more visibility into the assault on the Capitol, even as it was taking place" than had been previously known.[14] The head of the Proud Boys, Enrique Tarrio, was previously an FBI informant (though whether he continued this relationship into January 6th is unknown).[15] So was Joe Biggs, another Proud Boy leader convicted for his role in the initial breach.[16] And the vice president of the Oath Keepers, the other main militia group blamed for January 6th, was similarly a longtime FBI informant.[17] At a certain point one wonders who, among these groups, *didn't* have a relationship with the FBI!

Informants weren't the only way the government was able to anticipate in advance how January 6th might turn out. They were monitoring social media communications in real time. Just look at the so-called Norfolk memo, a threat assessment written up on January 5 by analysts at the

FBI's office in Norfolk, Virginia. The memo covered multiple threats, such as a post online to "Be ready to fight. Congress needs to hear glass breaking, doors being kicked in . . . Go there ready for war." The threats were so significant that Donell Harvin, head of intelligence at Washington, D.C.'s homeland security fusion center (the name given to an operation involving multiple agencies) urged officials to prepare for a "mass casualty event," calling on D.C.-area hospitals to empty their ERs and stock up on blood.[18] According to a *Washington Post* write-up, alarm bells at multiple intelligence fusion centers throughout the country went off, and "the date, hour, and location of concern was the same—1:00 P.M., U.S. Capitol, January 6th."

Given this advanced knowledge, it is odd that the federal authorities did not think to intervene or even implement heightened security protocols. Even without such advanced knowledge one would have suspected heightened security protocols near the Capitol, given the controversial certification proceeding taking place. Instead, the Capitol seemed to suffer from uniquely poor security that day. The generous reading is that authorities were simply caught flat-footed. Of course, if this is the case it calls into question the efficacy of the constitutionally questionable techniques the government uses to surveil American citizens and aggressively infiltrate politically incorrect groups. A less charitable reading is that authorities may have simply wanted something to happen on January 6th in order to justify a massive clampdown on Trump supporters. A still less charitable view is that elements of the government may have actively helped to instigate chaos on January 6th.

Readers who might be scandalized by the suggestion of governmental foul play on January 6th need only look at the long history of government malfeasance to assist their intuitions. We could look back to the days of FBI director J. Edgar Hoover, but there's no need. As recently as October 2020, FBI infiltration into politically incorrect groups has tainted prosecutions of their members. I'm talking, of course, about the Gretchen

VIVEK RAMASWAMY

Whitmer kidnapping plot. As you may recall, just prior to the 2020 election, a group of so-called militia extremists were arrested for allegedly planning to kidnap the Michigan governor Gretchen Whitmer.

Immediately one can discern striking parallels with January 6th. Though the Whitmer plot is often called a "kidnapping plot," it also involved alleged plans to storm the Michigan capitol building. In addition, many of the plotters were involved in the Three Percenters militia, one of the three main militia groups blamed for January 6th. The striking thing, however, is the level of government involvement in this alleged plot. Of the fourteen individuals originally involved in the alleged plot, at least five were either undercover agents or informants.[19]

Even more disturbing is the fact that every active step in this alleged plot was initiated and enabled by one of the agents or informants themselves. A careful look at the annotated indictment reveals that FBI operatives played the most important leadership role at every stage.[20] The plot's explosives expert, whom the plotters were supposed to buy explosives from, was an FBI agent. The head of transportation for the militia outfit turned out to be an undercover FBI agent. The head of security turned out to be an undercover FBI informant. At least three undercover FBI informants were active participants in the initial meeting in which the plot to storm the Michigan Capitol was allegedly hatched—meaning the FBI infiltrated before the conspiracy even began.

In a representative example of a reconnaissance mission of Whitmer's home, three out of five people in the van were either FBI agents or informants—that's 60 percent, for those keeping track. Worse, the FBI-informant ringleader convinced the other defendants to go on the recon mission by telling him they were out hunting pedophiles, not scoping out the possible kidnapping location. When he told his FBI handler that the ride-along was based on false pretenses, his handler threatened him: "If you stick with the story that [the militia members were] out there on a pedophile ring, you'll be a star witness in the defense.[21] There's zero options for that."

By the time the trial came around, two of the main FBI agents ended up having to recuse themselves from the case, which was so dirty that the judge approved an entrapment defense for several defendants, and the initial trials of four key defendants failed to produce a single conviction—a striking and embarrassing result for the government.

"In America, the FBI is not supposed to create domestic terrorists so that the FBI can arrest them," one of the defense lawyers explained during closing arguments.[22] No kidding. In all, the government was able to secure just five guilty verdicts (five were acquitted, and four took plea deals). Even those raise significant constitutional concerns.[23] The defendants were never allowed to call the FBI informant ringleader to testify, for example, because he pled the Fifth.[24] The FBI, you see, never wanted him to testify. In fact, they never even wanted to admit he was an informant—he had a rap sheet longer than a CVS receipt, including sex with a minor, selling guns, and drug dealing—so the FBI decided to call him "another individual" rather than a confidential informant in the indictment, and then threatened to prosecute him on more gun charges if he stepped too far out of line.[25] But no worries: "The government is allowed to induce somebody to commit a crime, so long as they're predisposed to commit that crime," one law professor explained to the *Wall Street Journal* after the verdict.[26]

As it so happens, the person in charge of the FBI's Detroit field office who oversaw the Whitmer operation was a man called Steven D'Antuono. Just a day after the initial arrests of the alleged Whitmer plotters in October 2020, FBI director Christopher Wray handpicked D'Antuono for a coveted spot running Washington, D.C.'s FBI field office. In fact, D'Antuono was the head of the FBI's investigation into the January 6th pipe bombs! Why, of all FBI agents in the country, Christopher Wray would choose the man who had just overseen the Whitmer Kidnapping entrapment plot to head the D.C. Field office in the critical months leading up to and after January 6th, I leave as an exercise for the reader. [27]

THE PATH FORWARD: FREE SPEECH

Now, before the mainstream media jumps to dismiss the foregoing publicly available facts as a "conspiracy theory," allow me to reiterate: Based on what we know today, do we have definitive proof that the events of January 6th were orchestrated by FBI agents who incited mob violence to imprison Trump supporters? No, of course we don't.

But the questions are worth asking. And in a free and open society, we would be able to ask them. Today, of course, we cannot. In a well-functioning republic, the government would be transparent in sharing all information with the public about matters of public importance. Today, of course, our government does no such thing.

The sixteen members of Congress who have pushed for information and questioned the work of the January 6th committee have been dismissed as "conspiracy theorists" or just plain "bonkers"; an FBI agent had his security clearance revoked simply for sharing (not even endorsing) an article questioning the official narrative.[28] Rather than welcome transparency and open debate, the response is to simply denounce anyone who dares to ask questions.

So how do we balance the competing interests of ensuring that the public is well informed and not suckered into *conspiracism*, while also ensuring that the charge of conspiracism isn't used to suppress uncomfortable facts about governmental and institutional dishonesty? The best solution is to restore arguably the most important founding ideal of our nation in the first place: free speech.

In recent years, the public discourse around free speech often has often gotten lost in the minutiae of fringe examples of speech that *don't* enjoy

First Amendment protections. The proverbial example that is cited so often that it's grown stale is a reference to Justice Oliver Wendell Holmes's famous quip in *Schenk v. United States* that you can't yell "FIRE!" in a crowded theater. You're not free to menacingly threaten someone that you'll kill them; that's an illegal threat. You're not free to tell someone you're selling them a bottle of medicine when in fact it's snake oil; that's commercial fraud. You're not free to knowingly say something that is false and damaging about another person; that's defamation.

But the obsessive public focus in recent years on what you *can't* say has distorted our common understanding of what the First Amendment is really all about. Here it is in a nutshell: *the First Amendment protects all opinions.* There's really no exception to that rule.

The main reason our Founders enshrined free speech in the *First* Amendment to the Constitution is to protect individual liberty: you're not really free at all if you don't have the freedom to say what you believe. The ability to express your own opinions is arguably the most basic human right. As Justice John Marshall once explained, "The First Amendment serves not only the needs of the polity, but also those of the human spirit—a spirit that demands self-expression."[29] In the United States of America, it's your birthright; it always has been.

But individual liberty isn't the only reason that free speech is important. Free speech is also the path to truth. As the Supreme Court has explained, "the theory of our Constitution is that the best test of truth is the power of the thought to get itself accepted in the competition of the market."[30] The remedy for false speech is true speech; the cure for irrational speech is rational speech. As President Trump recently wrote in a legal brief in the Twitter Files case, in which he sued the Biden administration and Twitter for censoring his posts:

[C]rackpot ideas sometimes turn out to be true. The earth does revolve around the sun, and it was Hunter Biden, not Russian disinformation agents, who dropped off a laptop full of incriminating evidence at a repair shop in Delaware. Galileo spent his remaining days under house arrest for spreading heretical ideas, and thousands of dissidents today are arrested or killed by despotic governments eager to suppress ideas they disapprove of. But this is not the American way. We believe the path to truth is forged by exposing all ideas to opposition, debate and discussion. Confident in the wisdom of the American people, we believe ideas that survive the gauntlet of criticism will flourish and those that don't will fall by the wayside. $E=mc^2$ revolutionized physics, not because it got thousands of likes on Facebook, but because it survived withering criticism by proclaimed experts.

Trump's comparison to science is apt. The scientific method, for example, depends on free speech and open debate: empirical testing requires a hypothesis to test in the first place, yet the generation of those hypotheses is really just an exercise in expressing *opinions*. You can't know what's true unless you have the freedom to express opinions that may be wrong—and to rule it out through others expressing their own competing opinions as well.

Free speech is the ultimate precondition for holding the government accountable. The ability of citizens to engage in criticizing their government is the only way that government can ultimately be held accountable to its citizens. Sure, elections matter too—citizens can vote bad actors out of office if they do a bad job. But you can only really *know* they're doing a bad job if citizens are free to point that out and express their opinions about it in the first place. Without that, the act of casting a vote at the ballot box is meaningless. It's just going through the motions.

We likely wouldn't know that Omar al-Bayoumi was an alleged Saudi spy, or that Covid-19 did indeed originate in a lab in China, or that the Trump-Russia collusion allegations were false, or that the Hunter Biden laptop story doesn't seem to have been "disinformation," unless citizens were free to question the initial narratives they were fed. It's no different when the subject matter becomes more uncomfortable or topical—like understanding the truth of what happened on January 6, 2021. The questions that seem beyond the pale to ask today are, from the vantage point of tomorrow, the ones that were vital to get to the truth.

There's another practical danger to the suppression of opinions. If you tell people they cannot speak, that is when they scream. But if you tell people they cannot *scream*, that's when they start tearing things down. It's ironic that public inquiry around the unanswered questions relating to January 6th is suppressed, because it was arguably the systematic suppression of speech in the year 2020—on topics ranging from Covid lockdowns to the origin of the virus to BLM-led riots, to the Hunter Biden laptop story—that culminated in the events of January 6, 2021. If we make the same mistakes, we are doomed for worse in the future.

Liberty. Truth. Peace. It turns out that all three go together, and free speech is the through line that connects them. Our Founders understood that deeply. We would be well served to understand it once more today. And the Constitution is the single greatest protector of that aspect of individual liberty—and many others—in all of human history. Like the rights it guarantees, however, the Constitution itself is now under attack.

FIVE TRUTHS

1. The term *conspiracy theorist* is now wielded in the same manner as terms like *racist, homophobe,* and *climate denier*—as a way to silence legitimate dissent rather than to engage with it directly.
2. We now know definitively that Saudi nationals and intelligence agents were involved in the 9/11 attacks, but saying so remains outside the Overton Window of acceptable public debate in both parties—*not* because it is false, but because it's viewed as disruptive to modern foreign policy goals.

3. Government actors and other institutions purposefully dismissed the lab-leak theory for the origin of Covid-19—*not* because it was false, but because it was viewed as disruptive to public trust and obeisance during the early stages of the pandemic.

4. We should rightly ask the question of what is dismissed *today* as a "conspiracy theory" that will be widely accepted as true in the future. Timing is often everything: while it is perfectly safe and uncontroversial to suggest *now* that Covid-19 came from a lab in China, the moment when it would have had the greatest positive impact on policy decisions has long passed.

5. The path to truth runs through free speech and open debate. Silencing dissent fosters more conspiracism, not less.

10

THE U.S. CONSTITUTION IS THE STRONGEST GUARANTOR OF FREEDOM IN HISTORY

The United States Constitution is under attack.

If you're a regular consumer of the *New York Times* or MSNBC, you might know this (also, congratulations on making it to the final chapter of this book; I hope you've learned something). Every few months, another op-ed or news analysis piece runs in mainstream media outlets declaring that our Constitution is outdated, broken, or in need of serious revamping if it's going to continue to serve the people.

In August 2022, two Ivy League professors—one from Harvard, the other from Yale—argued in an article titled "The Constitution Is Broken and Should Not Be Reclaimed" that "constitutions—especially the broken one we have now—inevitably orient us to the past and misdirect the present into a dispute over what people agreed on once upon a time, not on what the present and future demand for and from those who live now.[1] This aids the right, which insists on sticking with what it claims to be the original meaning of the past."

Their suggestion, which wasn't nearly as radical as they seemed to believe, was that we redesign our entire system of government to reflect the will of the people—whatever it happens to be at the time. Throughout the history of the United States, we've seen this argument pop up repeatedly, usually from those on the political left. Supreme Court justices with a liberal bent often talk about the Constitution as a "living document," which should change according to the shifting attitudes of the age. Democratic politicians talk about abandoning the structure of our government to "pack" the Supreme Court with more justices, a move that would allow them to get more favorable outcomes on their pet issues.

Of all the bad ideas we've discussed in this book, abandoning the Constitution—or even deviating from it—might be the most dangerous one.

For some reason, it has become controversial to defend our founding documents in public. Part of the answer, I'm sure, has to do with the fact that the Constitution did not explicitly prohibit slavery, nor did it grant full and equal rights to women. However, the document laid the *foundation* for the United States to make progress on both fronts. It's no accident that when Martin Luther King Jr. and his supporters marched on Washington, D.C., in 1963, they were *quoting* the Constitution, not denigrating it. In Dr. King's own words, he had come to Washington to "cash a check," that check being the promises afforded to all people by the United States Constitution.

The modern left, however, believes in revolutionary change, and so demands abandoning the core document that governs our society. They believe that as society improves, it outgrows the need for the strict rules set forth in our Constitution. However, to quote the great Supreme Court justice Antonin Scalia, these people say this "as if societies only ever improve over time, like they never *rot*." It is ridiculous to believe, especially given all the evidence of societal collapse we've seen over the last few hundred pages, that society always moves "forward."

Change is not always good. Some societal changes reflect a deviation from truth, the opposite of progress—or at least the kind of progress that is worthy. We require a North Star, a fixed set of commitments from the past to find our way back toward what is right. *That* is why we have a Constitution. The catalysts for "progress" in our country are manifold, and it's fair to admit that the Constitution isn't one of them. That's not its job. Rather the Constitution is a *conservative* document in the most literal sense of the word: it aims to *conserve* certain fixed principles over time, even in the face of ever-changing circumstances.

That's also why the Constitution is undemocratic in certain ways. That might sound strange, but it was *designed* to be that way. The document expressly enumerates rights that the will of the people cannot overturn— even if a majority wish to do so at a given moment. Under our Constitution, no matter how many people want to pass a law making it legal to inflict cruel and unusual punishments like torture, it can't happen, because the Eighth Amendment says so. No matter how many people vote to curtail the freedom to express heinous opinions, or to abolish the practice of offensive religions, it can't happen; the First Amendment says so. No matter how many people wish to adopt a national ban on guns, it can't happen; the Second Amendment says so. No matter how urgent the circumstance to arrest a criminal at large, the government can't search a house or car of a person without probable cause; the Eighth Amendment says so. The temptation to alter these rights can often be great. That's why our Founders worked so hard to ensure that the document was immune to majoritarian whims.

A careful reader of this entire book might call me a hypocrite for now defending these antimajoritarian aspects of the Constitution. It's true that I argued vehemently in chapter 5 against the existence of the modern administrative state, on *democratic* grounds. That was a central premise of my candidacy for president: the people we elect to run the government *should be the ones who actually run the government,* not the unelected bureaucrats who issue most binding edicts today. Defenders of the administrative state argue that technically savvy, expert bureaucrats are required to blunt the impact of whimsical populist impulses for the betterment of people. It's a kind of elite benevolence that might be antidemocratic but supposedly still works to benefit our nation's citizenry overall. On the face of it, doesn't my defense of the antimajoritarian aspects of the Constitution contradict my criticism of the antidemocratic aspects of the administrative state?

No—and here's why. The heart of my criticism of the modern administrative state wasn't just that it's antidemocratic. It's that it's *unconstitutional.* Certain safeguards are indeed required to protect against majoritarian incursions on individual liberties. That's what the Constitution achieves, both through the inviolable individual rights enshrined in the Bill of Rights as well as in the checks and balances and separation of government powers enshrined in the first four articles of the Constitution. By contrast, the administrative state is fundamentally hostile to individual liberty. It uses extra-constitutional means of lawmaking and enforcement to restrain individual behavior. It sidesteps the parts of the Constitution that *are* designed to preserve and protect democratic accountability for those whom we elect to make laws and enforce them. If your priority is to guarantee basic human freedoms, then embracing the antimajoritarian protections in the Bill of Rights and the democratic accountability codified in the way we pass laws through Congress are equally important. The administrative state is anathema to both.

Throughout our history, the Constitution's rigidity has allowed for greater human freedom than any other document in the history of mankind. The freedom of speech enjoyed by citizens of the United States is unrivaled anywhere in the world, as is our right to bear arms and our privacy protections against a potentially tyrannical government.

You might object and say that other countries have constitutions that contain the same rights as those of the United States. In modern cases, that's because many of those countries took inspiration from the U.S. Constitution—so in those cases, it's true by definition. But in other cases, the rights often listed on a piece of paper are not always upheld. In the

Weimar Republic, for instance, German citizens wrote a constitution that was extremely progressive for its time, including civil rights protections, a welfare state, and provisions for a democratic government. The same was true in Czechoslovakia, Venezuela, and the Soviet Union. But these governments crumbled because there was no structure to uphold the high ideals set forth in their founding documents. Even today, nations from China to Iran profess to offer many of the same protections delineated in our own Bill of Rights. Yet neither one contains a Second Amendment, which is one of the many reasons why the other rights they claim to respect—such as freedom of speech—remain unprotected in practice in those countries.

Our Constitution enshrines a delicate balance. The document ordains three branches of the federal government, each of which contains constraints on the operation of the other; the entire federal government is limited by the principle of federalism, which reserves most lawmaking power to the states; the federal government and the states are together limited by the inviolable rights enumerated in the Bill of Rights and subsequent amendments. Despite the problems outlined in this book, this balance usually works to preserve individual liberty—certainly more so than in any other nation known to the history of man.

Our contemporary problem *isn't* the Constitution. It's that we're failing to follow it—because we misunderstand it, lawmakers and ordinary citizens alike. A recent farcical example illustrates the point. It begins, as so many ridiculous things do, on a college campus.

MISUNDERSTANDINGS

In the spring of 2024, for the second time in five years, the university-wide commencement ceremony at Columbia University was canceled. So too were many other commencements at universities across the country.

It wasn't Covid-19, a pathogen of the respiratory system, that was responsible this time. It was, to borrow a phrase from the evolutionary psychologist Gad Saad, a pathogen of the *mind.*

For weeks leading up to the graduation ceremonies, students filed out onto the quads of these campuses—most notably Columbia, which sits on a quiet patch of land on the Upper West Side of Manhattan—and set up tents. In the minds of these students, they were waging a battle in their own home surroundings that would raise awareness of a problem that U.S. leaders were willfully ignoring: Israel's persecution of the Palestinian people.

According to conservative media's telling of it, Gen Z has been so infected by this woke mind virus (a pithy phrase often attributed to Elon Musk) that such behaviors on college campuses in 2024 was the inevitable result of years of an educational system that *pushed* anti-American ideologies onto American children over the course of two decades. And if this is what today's college students believe, it's the inevitable precursor of what America will soon become.

That's a gloomy picture indeed. There's undoubtedly some truth to it too. But take it from someone who wrote an earlier book about the spread of wokeism in America: this standard conservative account of the 2024 campus protests misses the mark.

What I saw in those campus protests *wasn't* a group of students who were cynically using the Palestinian flag to avoid their spring exams—in the way that countless corporations flaunted BLM flags to duck scrutiny for unrelated corporate malfeasance. These students weren't cynical at all.

But they weren't quite genuine either. Unlike the antiwar protestors during the Vietnam War—who stood up out of principle and self-interest against a draft that was sending America's sons to fight a losing war on the other side of the world—the 2024 campus protestors had very little

---

* *Gad Saad's book* The Parasitic Mind *was published in October 2020.*

idea what exactly they were even protesting. "From the river to the sea," they screamed, without the first clue of which river or which sea they were referring to. They protested for Palestinian statehood, yet most couldn't find Gaza or the West Bank on a map. In one revealing instance, students were vehemently heard chanting *intifada*, the Arab word for "uprising"—except a careful listen to the footage in one instance reveals they were actually saying "Infi-tada," which isn't even a word in Arabic or any other known language. Video footage of the event, circulated widely on Fox News, confirms that despite demonstrating such moral fervor, most of the protestors were totally ignorant. They were uttering sounds without knowing what they meant, or what they were even *intended* to mean.

To be either cynical or genuine, you must know what your intentions actually *are*. The 2024 campus protestors were neither of these things. Like so many Americans, they were just *lost*. First it was the BLM flag; next it was the transgender flag; next it was the Ukraine flag; now it was the Palestinian flag. They are hungry to be part of something bigger than themselves, but they can't even answer what it means to be an American.

To be clear, they *believed* they were exercising their American birthright of free speech. But the First Amendment protects the expression of opinions, not the right to stop other people from attending classes or expressing their own. In order to know the difference, you have to know something basic about the constitution of your nation. While many of those protestors who interrupted classes and commencement ceremonies surely thought of themselves as defenders of constitutional rights as they resisted forcible removal, they in fact knew very little.

Yet as often happens, the legislative reaction in response to the madness was even more egregious.

The First Amendment *does* protect the expression of all opinions, something that 197 House Republicans forgot entirely when they joined Democrats to pass the "Antisemitism Awareness Act." The campus protests became a catalyst to rush through a piece of legislation that adopted the

International Holocaust Remembrance Alliance's definition of antisemitism, and then *banned the expressions of opinions* encompassed by that definition. That is, the U.S. government effectively outsourced our speech policies to an NGO that historically has taken political stances. That bill passed the House by a margin of 320–91 and is being considered in the Senate as this book goes to print.

Like many campus protestors who had little idea what they were actually chanting, many congressmen who voted for this act surely had no idea what it actually said, just as they have no idea what many of the bills they vote for actually say. It's equally clear that the First Amendment *doesn't* protect blockading students from going to class and *does* protect the expression of the opinions that Congress is trying to ban. On the question of what the Constitution actually says, Republicans and Democrats increasingly compete for the prize of which party is *more* lost.

I have no doubt that this bill—if enacted into law—would be struck down by the Supreme Court, perhaps even 9–0, if challenged. Still, it would be nice if our elected officials were more educated in what our Constitution actually says, and what its words mean. We would certainly be able to save a little time if bills could be dismissed out of hand because they violated some principle of the Constitution.

We don't need to reinvent who we are as Americans. All we need to do is to rediscover it.

THE FACTS

The Declaration of Independence is the greatest mission statement for a nation in human history. Right from the second paragraph, it lays out truths that have held up over the centuries:

> We hold these truths to be self-evident, that all men are created
> equal, that they are endowed by their Creator with certain unal-

ienable Rights, that among these are Life, Liberty and the pursuit of Happiness.—That to secure these rights, Governments are instituted among Men, deriving their just powers from the consent of the governed,—That whenever any Form of Government becomes destructive of these ends, it is the Right of the People to alter or to abolish it, and to institute new Government, laying its foundation on such principles and organizing its powers in such form, as to them shall seem most likely to effect their Safety and Happiness.

If the Declaration is our mission statement, then the U.S. Constitution is our operating manual. Unlike countries like Iran and China that *claim* to protect free speech, our Framers understood that the First Amendment is meaningless without the Second Amendment to actualize it. They understood that the Bill of Rights were still a set of *amendments* to a basic structure of government with a carefully calibrated set of checks and balances to ensure that leaders are accountable directly to the public. They understood that even though the ten amendments they initially adopted protected the rights that they felt were most important, they ordained a process for amending that entire document, a process that yielded momentous changes in subsequent years that they didn't countenance at the time of our Founding—from suffrage for women to the emancipation of slaves.

How do we fix the egregious lack of public understanding of these basic principles? During my presidential campaign, I advanced avant-garde policies ranging from the abolition of the Department of Education to the requirement that high school students pass the same civics test required of naturalized citizens before casting a ballot.

I stand by these policies, but I'm increasingly convinced we can't just revive the founding principles enshrined in the Constitution by preaching them—or even mandating their education. We too easily forget the fact that the Revolutionary War—and the Constitutional Convention that followed it—took place against the backdrop of a founding *culture* in America.

It was a founding culture defined by the special combination of courage and curiosity. That's what we really miss today.

Consider who were some of the most intellectually groundbreaking thinkers of the eighteenth century. You might be tempted to cite the likes of Jefferson and Washington, but they *weren't* among them. Rather most of them were on the other side of the Atlantic. They were the likes of Locke, Rousseau, and Montesquieu who led the way in philosophy; Newton and Leibniz who led in math and physics; Adam Smith and David Hume in economics and psychology.

The thing that distinguished our Founding Fathers wasn't their genius in any of these disciplines. They weren't mathematical or philosophical savants; they just learned from the people who were. The thing that really distinguished them was their ability to combine those intellectual foundations with a vision for the future that simply didn't exist in the Old World.

Minds like Locke and Leibniz, Newton and Hume, were hands-down brilliant. But the European society in which they were born was different from ours in a fundamental way: they valued expertise over curiosity. They stayed in their lanes. The people who were supposed to run the government . . . ran the government. The people who were supposed to philosophize about the government . . . philosophized about it. But they weren't the same people.

The Old World was fundamentally reluctant to break down boundaries. Boundaries, they thought, existed for a reason. The ruling class existed to rule; the expert class existed to advise them.

But our Founding Fathers were different. They didn't believe in those boundaries. They didn't even really believe in the necessity of expertise.

Take the case of Benjamin Franklin, one of the coauthors of the Declaration of Independence. He was a polymath genius, who in addition to founding universities and hospitals was also a prolific author, a dabbler in medicine who discovered a treatment of the common cold, and a creator of musical instruments—including one instrument that went on to be used by Mozart and Beethoven. Some of his devices were incredibly practical, such as the lightning rod for the home, the bifocal glasses, and the Franklin stove—a tool for heating food in the house, but also a major breakthrough in the field of thermodynamics. Franklin was the archetype of the eighteenth-century Renaissance man. Most people with a basic understanding of American history know most of these facts about him.

But here's the remarkable part: Franklin wasn't an exception. His level of intellectual curiosity was actually the *norm*. Take two of his lesser-known cosigners of the Declaration. Robert Livingston designed the steamship, the fundamental building block of the Industrial Revolution, as a side project, while serving as an ambassador to France. Roger Sherman was a self-educated attorney who never actually went to law school, someone who had no formal education but who was so committed to ensuring the education of the next generation of Americans that he ended up serving on the governing body of Yale.

And of course, there were the two most famous signatories of that document—John Adams and Thomas Jefferson, who together formed one of the great intellectual rivalries in human history. Jefferson was more of a scientist; Adams was more of a humanities guy. But they were each deeply curious about the home turf of the other, and unafraid to compete with a true heavyweight.

"I must study politics and war," Adams once said, "that our sons may have liberty to study mathematics and philosophy."

It's true that Adams studied politics and war, but he also studied math and philosophy. And poetry, Greek, and Latin. In fact, a little-known detail about John Adams is that after serving as our second president, he committed himself to becoming a scholar of Hindu scripture. He said that if he were to live his life again, he'd have been a Sanskrit scholar. John Adams was a lifelong learner.

And so was his nemesis, Thomas Jefferson. The man was fluent in five languages and capable of reading two more. Over the course of his life, he wrote sixteen thousand letters. A contemporary student reading that might run the mental math. You know, 16,000 letters . . . that's like 4,000 words, which is like 5 whole pages, double-spaced . . . which probably seems like a lot to a college kid who's busy chanting "Infi-Tada" on the campus lawn. But no, I don't mean that Thomas Jefferson wrote 16,000 letters of the alphabet by hand. I mean that he wrote over 16,000 full essays by hand.

You might wonder if it was uncomfortable for him to sit in a chair for so long while writing. Well, it turns out he solved that problem too by inventing the polygraph and the swivel chair, which he built and sat in while writing the Declaration of Independence. The Virginia State Capitol, standing right there in Richmond to this day, was designed by Thomas Jefferson.

There was something in the water back then, something in the *culture*. It was a culture that valued education, autodidacts, exploration, a fundamental curiosity about how the world works, and an unyielding confidence that even if you weren't an expert in something, you could still figure it out with the right combination of self-education and curiosity.

Compared to nations like France and England, it's true that America was provincial at the time. We were nothing more than a backwater cluster of small towns scattered along the eastern seaboard. Economically, militarily, and geopolitically, it seemed that we were destined to be nothing more than a footnote in global history. Yet the people who wrote those footnotes were deeply curious about the world they inhabited, and about the history to which they contributed; they were also deeply confident in their ability to change every part of it for the better. And that's exactly what they did.

We need to revive that special combination of curiosity and confidence. Yes, we want to be a country of people who tinker in their garages. We want people who write great essays in the evenings, while working as mechanics or business owners during the day. We should expect more of one another as citizens. We should expect more of ourselves. We should expect more of our leaders. Back then, presidents who left the White House went on to become scholars of Sanskrit; today they sign Netflix deals and retire on Martha's Vineyard.

It's easy to say "how cool were our Founding Fathers," and then go back to the daily drudgery of our modern technocracy. But why can't we behave like them too? Conservatives talk a lot about staying true to the political and legal principles in the Constitution, and no doubt that's important. But as Americans, we should also be inspired to stay true to our founding culture of exploration, irreverence, and curiosity. *Without that, we're not even equipped to understand what our Constitution even means.* That's how you get to "pro-Palestine" campus activists blockading college buildings thinking that their physical transgressions are constitutionally protected. That's how you get to Republican congressmen banning the nonviolent expression of opinions in the name of an "Antisemitism Awareness Act."

The irony is that it should be a lot easier for us to do that today than it was for them back then. For starters, the main languages of scholarship in 1776 were French and Latin, and you had to wait weeks or even months to get a physical copy of a book that you might have wanted to read. Today almost everything is available in any language you want, and you're two swipes on your iPhone away from any book you want to read on demand. The only thing stopping us is our own incuriosity, our own veneration of someone else's expertise, and our own lack of confidence to build our own.

You might expect that our Founding Fathers didn't have the time to afford the luxuries of intellectual curiosity. They were struggling for their own survival against the British Empire. Yet actually, the opposite was true. The culture of England was less curious and less confident at its core. That's why they lost; that's why we won. That's why they've been in decline in the 250 years since then; that's why we went on to become the greatest nation in modern history. The special sauce that allowed America to succeed was our Founding Fathers' unique brew of curiosity combined with confidence.

And it wasn't just a matter of self-indulgence. The reason our Founding Fathers were so curious about the world around them wasn't just to get drunk on it. It's because they strived to make America, their nation, a better nation. It wasn't idle interest that moved them; it was a desire to create a thriving nation that would outlive them.

And thrive that nation did. They made our nation a magnet for minds that were as curious and courageous as their own. One of the most important chemists of the eighteenth century was Joseph Priestley, a British guy who had unusual religious beliefs that defied mainstream Anglican thought. It soon became unsafe for him to remain in England, so he moved to Pennsylvania, where he was welcomed by the likes of Franklin and Jefferson. It may have been the first notable example of a brilliant scientist moving to America precisely because we're a free society, a tradition that so many others, including my own mother and father, followed centuries later. My parents came here for the same reason that Priestley did, in search of a free society where creative people are able to pursue their dreams however they see fit.

Priestley set sail for the United States in 1794, just five years after the Constitution went into effect. That's no coincidence: that's the document that codified his reason for making the journey.

Priestley didn't come to America because we had great universities, or funding for his research; in fact, we had neither of those things back then. It's because here he had freedom. The freedom to explore ideas without fear of being locked up. Freedom to be himself, including even the freedom to discover who he was. That's the unspoken part of the American

Dream, not just the freedom to achieve whatever you want, but also the freedom to discover what it is you want to achieve.

It's precisely when we stopped being insurgents and became incumbents that we lost that sense of curiosity and of confidence. And if we don't change course, we'll become the incumbent unseated by a backwater nation on the other side of another ocean.

The way we remain a magnet for the most curious and ambitious people around the world is by cultivating the culture that drew Joseph Priestley here. A culture that prizes free and open debate and inquiry; a culture that doesn't force a monolithic cultural ideology on everyone; a culture that doesn't force you to bow down to what a politically appointed expert says on a given day, but instead gives you the latitude to question dogmas in the pursuit of truth.

That's the greatest thing our Founding Fathers invented. It wasn't a lightning rod or a stove. It was a country that offered freedom of thought, the greatest invention that produced so many others. That's the invention we risk losing in a country that focuses on suppressing dissent instead of fostering creativity. Can we sustain that special combination of curiosity and confidence? That's the defining question of our era—and the answer starts with reviving the ideals in our Constitution and culminates in how we pass those values on to the next generation.

Those who object to this vision as the exclusive North Star for educating our children will say that it's not enough for our schools and universities to teach our children to be intellectually curious, courageous, and confident—that we must also teach them to be socially just, and to rectify the injustices created by the likes of our Founding Fathers, who blindly pursued enlightenment without actually abiding by the values that they preached.

I would argue precisely the opposite. Intellectual curiosity and courage, combined with a willingness to traverse boundaries that go beyond your preordained area of "expertise," beyond your own "lane," is the most important building block of empathy. And empathy is the most important building block of justice, something that 2024's wave of Infi-Tada chanters would do well to remember.

The soil is more fertile now to plant those seeds than I've seen over the past decade. There's a wave of young people who have tired of false idols and are moving on. On the campus of the University of North Carolina, a group of fraternity brothers proudly stood around the American flag, holding it up even as a group of Hamas-supporting protestors attempted to take it down. At a frat party on the campus of Stanford University, another group of students stood up and spontaneously began singing the national anthem. These events weren't covered widely by the mainstream media, of course, which leads me to believe that they are far more common than you might think.

Our Founders were a band of renegade rebels. It's nice to see America's youth start to *actually* rebel again. They are hungry to be part of something bigger themselves, just as we all are. We don't need false identities to fill that void. All we need is to seek the same thing our Founders did in 1776: the truth.

FIVE TRUTHS

1. The modern left is increasingly skeptical of the Constitution, an uncomfortable fact that quietly underlies many contemporary U.S. political debates.
2. Democrats aren't alone at fault: Republicans are often complicit in abandoning the Constitution to implement short-run political goals as a reactionary response to left-wing excess.
3. The Constitution's antimajoritarian rigidity isn't a bug, it's a feature. Critics argue for a "living Constitution" that adapts to contemporary values, but the value of the Constitution is that no matter how many

people desire to pass a law that violates one of its protections, they cannot.

4. The unique balance of powers and rights enshrined in the Constitution has allowed it to uphold human freedoms more effectively than any other governing document in history.

5. Preserving the ideals enshrined in the Constitution requires reviving the founding *culture* that produced it—including attributes like curiosity, irreverence, and insurgence. The next generation of Americans appears as hungry as ever for that cultural revival.

ACKNOWLEDGMENTS

I would like to acknowledge my friends Stephanie Solomon, Sean McGowan, Darren Beattie, Matt Luby, Tricia McLaughlin, Amanda Sweeney, and the entire team at Javelin, particularly Keith Urbahn and Megan Stencel, without whom this book and its rollout would not have been possible. Thank you to Threshold Editions for your courage to publish this book.

NOTES

INTRODUCTION

1. Christine Flowers, "NPR Leader Shows Her True Colors," *Longview News-Journal*, April 25, 2024, https://www.news-journal.com/opinion/columnists/flowers-npr-leader -shows-her-true-colors/article_3b83bc6a-024a-11ef-aed8-47205c8bf1fa.html.

CHAPTER ONE: GOD IS REAL

1. Jim Holt, *Why Does the World Exist? An Existential Detective Story*, (New York: Liveright, 2012).
2. Lawrence M. Krauss, *The Edge of Knowledge: Unsolved Mysteries of the Cosmos*, (New York: Atria Books, 2023).
3. Corey S. Powell, "Relativity Versus Quantum Mechanics: the Battle for the Universe," *The Guardian*, November 4, 2015, https://www.theguardian.com/news/2015 /nov/04/relativity-quantum-mechanics-universe-physicists.
4. "String Theory Is Dead," *EIN News*, February 22, 2023, https://www.einnews.com /pr_news/618684925/string-theory-is-dead.
5. Jason Pargin, "10 Things Christians and Atheists Can (and Must) Agree On," Cracked, December 16, 2007, https://www.cracked.com/article_15759_10-things -christians-atheists-can-and-must-agree-on.html.
6. Adam Cohen, "What the Monkeys Can Teach Humans About Making America Fairer," *The New York Times*, September 21, 2003, https://www.nytimes.com /2003/09/21/opinion/editorial-observer-what-the-monkeys-can-teach-humans -about-making-america-fairer.html.
7. Jeffrey Kluger, "Is Morality Innate?," *Time*, June 16, 2022, https://time .com/6187834/is-morality-innate/.
8. Hannah Grossman, and Maria Lencki, "Famous Atheist Says He Identifies as Cultural Christian, Horrified by Promotion of Islamic Holiday," Fox News, April 2, 2024, https://www.foxnews.com/media/famous-atheist-says-identifies-cultural-chris tian-horrified-promotion-islamic-holiday.
9. Richard Dawkins, Twitter Post, March 21, 2018, https://x.com/RichardDawkins /status/976474848330469376?ref_src=twsrc%5Etfw%7Ctwcamp%5Etweetem bed%7Ctwterm%5E976474848330469376%7Ctwgr%5E730a617874ec6309add 4ae07fd484ed6c86c717a%7Ctwcon%5Es1_&ref_url=https%3A%2F%2Fwww .aciprensa.com%2Fnoticias%2F69342%2Ffamoso-ateo-reconoce-que-no-se -debe-celebrar-una-europa-menos-cristiana.
10. Ayaan Hirsi Ali, "Why I Am Now A Christian," UnHerd, November 11, 2023, https://unherd.com/2023/11/why-i-am-now-a-christian/.
11. Ibid.

CHAPTER TWO: THE CLIMATE CHANGE AGENDA IS A HOAX

1. Sarah Beth Hensley and Oren Oppenheim, "Climate Change, Mental Health, and UFOs," ABC News, August 24, 2023, https://abcnews.go.com/Politics/climate -change-mental-health-ufos-moments-missed-1st/story?id=102533900.

2. Rebecca Lindsey, and Luann Dahlman, "Climate Change: Global Temperature," Climate.gov, January 18, 2024, https://www.climate.gov/news-features/understand ing-climate/climate-change-global-temperature.

3. Stephen Koonin, *Unsettled: What Climate Science Tells Us, What It Doesn't, and Why It Matters*, (New York: BenBella Books, 2021), 33.

4. "World of Change: Antarctic Sea Ice," NASA Earth Observatory, January 5, 2023, https://earthobservatory.nasa.gov/world-of-change/sea-ice-antarctic#:~=From%20 the%20start%20of%20satelliteyear%20to%20year%20around%20Antarctica.

5. Alex Epstein, *Fossil Future: Why Global Human Flourishing Requires More Oil, Coal, and Natural Gas—Not Less*, (New York: Portfolio, 2022), 23.

6. Epstein, 25.

7. Ibid.

8. Joe Barrett, "Ethanol Industry Wants to Bury Its Carbon, but Some Farmers Stand in the Way," *The Wall Street Journal*, August 6, 2022, https://www.wsj.com/articles/ethanol-in dustry-wants-to-bury-its-carbon-but-some-farmers-stand-in-the-way-11659787200.

9. "Our Letter to Chevron," Strive Asset Management, September 6, 2022, https:// www.strive.com/strive-asset-management-letter-to-chevron.

10. John Dvorak, "Volcano Myths and Rituals," *American Scientist* 95, no. 1 (January-February 2007), https://www.americanscientist.org/article/volcano-myths-and-rituals.

11. Mark Stevenson, "Ancient Child Sacrifices Found in Mexico," NBC News, April 18, 2007, https://www.nbcnews.com/id/wbna18164233.

CHAPTER THREE: "AN OPEN BORDER IS NOT A BORDER"

1. "How Many Would Really Come if Borders Were Open," Center for Immigration Studies, May 8, 2019, https://cis.org/Immigration-Studies/How-Many-Would-Really -Come-if-Borders-Were-Open.

2. "Diversity Visa (DV) Statistics," U.S. Department of State, https://travel.state.gov/content /dam/visas/Diversity-Visa/DVStatistics/DV-applicant-entrants-by-country-2019-2021.pdf.

3. "Sierra Leone Integrated Household Survey 2018," Statistics Sierra Leone, October 2019, https://www.statistics.sl/images/StatisticsSL/Documents/SLIHS2018/SLIHS _2018_New/sierra_leone_integrated_household_survey2018_report.pdf#:~:text =From%20SLIHS2018%2C%20the%20average%20household%20size%20for ,6%2C%20as%20compared%20to%205.6%20in%202011.

4. "RIVARS GARCIA v. GARLAND," https://caselaw.findlaw.com/court/us-10th-cir cuit/2120498.html.

5. Erin Blakemore, "WWII Jewish Refugee Ship St. Louis," History, June 4, 2019, https://www.history.com/news/wwii-jewish-refugee-ship-st-louis-1939.

6. Jonathan Blitzer, "The Dream Homes of Guatemalan Migrants," New Yorker, April 5, 2019, https://www.newyorker.com/news/dispatch/the-dream-homes-of-guatemalan-migrants.

7. Todd Bensman, "Guatemalans Admit They're Illegally Entering the U.S. to Get Big-

ger Houses, Not Flee Violence," *The Federalist*, March 10, 2020, https://thefederalist
.com/2020/03/10/guatemalans-admit-theyre-illegally-entering-the-u-s-to-get-bigger
-houses-not-flee-violence/.

8. Juan Montes, and Alicia A. Caldwell, "Men Looking for Work Drive Migrant Surge
at the U.S. Border," *Wall Street Journal*, March 24, 2021, https://www.wsj.com/arti
cles/men-looking-for-work-drive-migrant-surge-at-the-u-s-border-11616624482.

9. Jake Offenhaurtz, Patrick Orsagos, and Renata Brito, "Thousands more Mauritani-
ans are making their way to the US, thanks to a route spread on social media," AP
News, August 19, 2023, https://apnews.com/article/mauritania-immigration-west-af
rica-united-states-tiktok-route-bbef5afc25680ad7f2704afa76f44cea; Julie Turkewitz,
"Migrants Tiktok Darien Gap," *New York Times*, December 20, 2023, https://www
.nytimes.com/2023/12/20/world/americas/migrants-tiktok-darien-gap.html.

10. Elliot Spagat, "For many asylum seekers, flying to Mexico is ticket to the US," AP
News, February 10, 2022, https://apnews.com/article/immigration-arizona-united
-states-mexico-colombia-fb4f913f2c43c48c0f4ecade8b2c1913.

11. Ibid.

12. Sam Dolnick, "Immigrants May Be Fed False Stories to Bolster Asylum Pleas," *New
York Times*, July 11, 2011, https://www.nytimes.com/2011/07/12/nyregion/immi
grants-may-be-fed-false-stories-to-bolster-asylum-pleas.html.

13. Ibid.

14. "Judge Reports," TRAC Immigration, October 19, 2023, https://trac.syr.edu/immi
gration/reports/judgereports/.

15. Ibid.

16. "Immigration Detention in the United States by Agency," American Immigration
Council, January 2020, https://www.americanimmigrationcouncil.org/sites/default
/files/research/immigration_detention_in_the_united_states_by_agency.pdf.

17. "UK Asylum Seekers Fear Over Safety in Rwanda Under Deportation Law," *Hindustan
Times*, April 24, 2024, https://www.hindustantimes.com/world-news/uk-asylum-seek
ers-fear-over-safety-in-rwanda-under-deportation-law-101713968539065.html.

18. Lauren Mechling, "Birth Tourism Documentary: China-US Citizenship," *The
Guardian*, December 11, 2023, https://www.theguardian.com/tv-and-radio/2023
/dec/11/birth-tourism-documentary-china-us-citizenship; Jesusemen Oni, "Foreigners Seeking American Citizenship for Children Flout Law, Endanger Babies," VOA
News, December 6, 2016, https://www.voanews.com/a/foreigners-seeking-american
-citizenship-children-flout-law-endanger-babies/3626080.html.

19. Iulia Stashevska, "Mother Russia: South Florida Sees a Boom in Birth Tourism," AP
News, March 22, 2019, https://apnews.com/general-news-travel-161a0db2666044d
c8d42932edd9b9ce6.

20. Alan Gomez, "Canada's Merit-Based Immigration System Wins Trump's Praise,"
USA Today, March 1, 2017, https://www.usatoday.com/story/news/world/2017/03/01
/donald-trump-canada-immigration-system-merit-based/98594790/.

21. Julie Turkewitz, "Profits to Be Made in Treacherous Darien Gap," *New York Times*, September 16, 2023, https://static01.nyt.com/images/2023/09/16/nytfrontpage/scan.pdf.

22. Troy Nehls, and Greg Sindelar, "Venezuela Won't Take Its Criminals Back, So Why

Does Biden Keep Taking Them?," The Hill, March 21, 2024, https://thehill.com /opinion/immigration/4532281-venezuela-wont-take-its-criminals-back-so-why-does -biden-keep-taking-them/.

23. Mac McClelland, "How to Build a Perfect Refugee Camp," *New York Times*, February 13, 2014, https://www.nytimes.com/2014/02/16/magazine/how-to-build-a-perfect-refugee-camp.html.

24. Ibid; Helen Andrews, "The Rise and Fall of International Adoption," The American Conservative, December 16, 2023, https://www.theamericanconservative.com/the -rise-and-fall-of-international-adoption/.

25. "Flores Ruling," New York Times, https://graphics8.nytimes.com/packages/pdf/us /FloresRuling.pdf.

26. Ibid; Luciana Magalhaes, Samantha Pearson, and Michelle Hackman, "Desperate to Cross Into the U.S., Some Brazilians Create Phony Families," *Wall Street Journal*, May 8, 2022, https://www.wsj.com/articles/desperate-to-cross-into-the-u-s-some-brazil ians-create-phony-families-11652025729.

27. John Davis, "Border Crisis: CBP Fights Child Exploitation," U.S. Customs and Border Protection, January 4, 2022, https://www.cbp.gov/frontline/border-crisis-cbp -fights-child-exploitation.

28. "DHS OIG Report," U.S. Department of Homeland Security, February 8, 2022, https://www.oig.dhs.gov/sites/default/files/assets/2022-02/OIG-22-27-Feb22.pdf; "Hyde-Smith Cosponsors Bill Requiring Familial DNA Testing at the Southern Border," Senator Cindy Hyde-Smith, June 7, 2023, https://www.hydesmith.senate.gov /hyde-smith-cosponsors-bill-requiring-familial-dna-testing-southern-border.

CHAPTER FOUR: THERE ARE TWO GENDERS

1. Scottie Andrew, "JK Rowling Podcast Release: What to Know," CNN, February 22, 2023, https://www.cnn.com/2023/02/21/entertainment/jk-rowling-podcast-release -what-to-know-cec/index.html.

2. Ibid.

3. "JK Rowling Says She Will Not Be Intimidated by Trans Activists," *The Telegraph*, November 22, 2021, https://www.telegraph.co.uk/news/2021/11/22/jk-rowling -says-will-not-intimidated-trans-activists-targeted/.

4. Jonathan Kay, "The Campaign of Lies Against Journalist Jesse Singal and Why It Matters," *Quillette*, March 18, 2021, https://quillette.com/2021/03/18/the-campaign -of-lies-against-journalist-jesse-singal-and-why-it-matters/.

5. Christopher Wiggins, "X Bans Deadnaming and Misgendering," *Advocate*, March 1, 2024, https://www.advocate.com/news/x-bans-deadnaming-misgendering.

6. GLAAD, Twitter Post, February 15, 2023, https://twitter.com/glaad/status /1625854419102478338.

7. "Final Report," *Cass Review*, April 2024, https://cass.independent-review.uk/home /publications/final-report/.

8. Ryan Gaydos, "Joe Rogan Asks Riley Gaines about Lia Thomas and Sex in Girls Sports," Fox News, March 8, 2024, https://www.foxnews.com/sports/joe-rogan-asks -riley-gaines-lia-thomas-sex-girls.

9. Kristine Parks, "Oklahoma Transgender Student Charged with Assaulting Female High School Classmates in Bathroom," Fox News, December 16, 2022, https://www.foxnews.com/media/oklahoma-transgender-student-charged-assaulting-female-high-school-classmates-bathroom.

10. "Transgender Wyoming Woman Convicted of Sexually Assaulting 10-Year-Old Girl in Bathroom," Fox News, October 19, 2017, https://www.foxnews.com/us/transgender-wyoming-woman-convicted-of-sexually-assaulting-10-year-old-girl-in-bathroom.

11. "Virginia Family Sues School System," AP News, October 6, 2023, https://apnews.com/article/loudoun-virginia-lawsuit-transgender-bathroom-sexual-assault-a26168568cc20c2aa6cec9bef50e7c3f.

12. "Interim Report, February 2024," Utah Legislature, February 2024, https://le.utah.gov/interim/2024/pdf/00000577.pdf.

13. Katherine Fung, "Democrats Help Republicans Ban Gender-Affirming Care for Transgender Kids," *Newsweek*, May 15, 2023, https://www.newsweek.com/democrats-help-republicans-ban-gender-affirming-care-transgender-kids-1800429.

14. Nazia Parveen, "Transgender Prisoner Who Sexually Assaulted Inmates Jailed for Life," *The Guardian*, October 11, 2018, https://www.theguardian.com/uk-news/2018/oct/11/transgender-prisoner-who-sexually-assaulted-inmates-jailed-for-life.

15. Kayley Whalen, "Invalidating Transgender Identities: Progress and Trouble in the DSM-5," National LGBTQ Task Force, December 13, 2012, https://www.thetaskforce.org/news/invalidating-transgender-identities-progress-and-trouble-in-the-dsm-5/.

CHAPTER FIVE: THERE ARE THREE BRANCHES OF U.S. GOVERNMENT, NOT FOUR

1. 1.SEC Rule 17a-4(b)(4).

2. Tarek J. Helou, Jessica Lonergan, and Nicholas E. Hakun, "Banks Fined $2 Billion for Employees' Off-Channel Communications: Is Your Industry at Risk?," Wilson Sonsini Goodrich & Rosati, November 16, 2022, https://www.wsgr.com/en/insights/banks-fined-dollar2-billion-for-employees-off-channel-communicationsis-your-industry-at-risk.html.

3. Gary S. Lawson, "The Rise and Rise of the Administrative State," Scholarly Commons at Boston University School of Law, 1994, https://scholarship.law.bu.edu/cgi/viewcontent.cgi?article=1941&context=faculty_scholarship.

CHAPTER SIX: THE NUCLEAR FAMILY IS THE GREATEST FORM OF GOVERNANCE KNOWN TO MANKIND

1. Brad Wilcox, "Elitism, Marriage Rates, and Hypocrisy," *The Atlantic*, February 13, 2024, https://www.theatlantic.com/ideas/archive/2024/02/elitism-marriage-rates-hypocrisy/677401/.

2. Wendy Wang, and W. Bradford Wilcox, "IFS State of Contradiction," Institute for Family Studies, 2020, https://archive.ph/o/97CL7/https://ifstudies.org/ifs-admin/resources/ifs-stateofcontradiction-final-1.pdf.

3. "The 2022 American Family Survey," Brookings Institution, 2022, https://archive.ph/o/97CL7/https://www.brookings.edu/events/the-2022-american-family-survey/.

4. Ed West, "Elites Don't Preach What They Practise," UnHerd, January 15, 2020, https://unherd.com/newsroom/elites-dont-preach-what-they-practise/.

5. "The Power of the Two-Parent Home," Clearly Reformed, May 27, 2022, https://clearlyreformed.org/the-power-of-the-two-parent-home/.

6. "America's Children: Family and Social Environment," ChildStats, https://www.childstats.gov/americaschildren/family2.asp; "The Two-Parent Privilege with Melissa Kearney," Niskanen Center, October 6, 2023, https://www.niskanencenter.org/the-two-parent-privilege-with-melissa-kearney/.

7. Stephanie Kramer, "U.S. Children More Likely than Children in Other Countries to Live with Just One Parent," Pew Research Center, December 12, 2019, https://www.pewresearch.org/short-reads/2019/12/12/u-s-children-more-likely-than-children-in-other-countries-to-live-with-just-one-parent/.

8. Dr. Joshua Coleman, "A Shift in American Family Values Is Fueling Estrangement," Dr. Joshua Coleman, January 10, 2021, https://www.drjoshuacoleman.com/post/a-shift-in-american-family-values-is-fueling-estrangement.

9. Sarah Jones, "Beyond the Nuclear Family," *Dissent Magazine*, Summer 2021, https://www.dissentmagazine.org/article/beyond-the-nuclear-family/.

10. Lara Bazelon, "Divorce and Children," *The New York Times*, September 30, 2021, https://www.nytimes.com/2021/09/30/opinion/divorce-children.html.

11. Joshua Coleman, "Why Parents and Kids Get Estranged," *The Atlantic*, January 10, 2021, https://www.theatlantic.com/family/archive/2021/01/why-parents-and-kids-get-estranged/617612/.

12. Brad Wilcox, "Elitism, Marriage Rates, and Hypocrisy," *The Atlantic*, February 13, 2024, https://www.theatlantic.com/ideas/archive/2024/02/elitism-marriage-rates-hypocrisy/677401/.

13. Dani Blum, "LGBTQ Chosen Families," *The New York Times*, June 25, 2022, https://www.nytimes.com/2022/06/25/well/lgbtq-chosen-families.html.

14. Dan Evon, "Blues Clues Pride Beaver Top Scars," Snopes, June 2, 2021, https://www.snopes.com/fact-check/blues-clues-pride-beaver-top-scars/; Lucy Diavolo, "Family-Friendly LGBTQ Pride: Chosen Families," *Teen Vogue*, June 14, 2021, https://www.teenvogue.com/story/family-friendly-lgbtq-pride-chosen-families.

15. "LGBTQ Paths to Parenthood," Family Equality, https://familyequality.org/lgbtq-paths-to-parenthood/; "13 Guiding Principles," DC Area Educators for Social Justice, https://www.dcareaeducators4socialjustice.org/black-lives-matter/13-guiding-principles/.

16. Seth Stephens-Davidowitz, "In the NBA, Zip Code Matters," *The New York Times*, November 2, 2013, https://www.nytimes.com/2013/11/03/opinion/sunday/in-the-nba-zip-code-matters.html.

17. Jeannine Mancini, "Jeff Bezos' Mom Was a Single Teen," Yahoo Finance, May 14, 2024, https://finance.yahoo.com/news/jeff-bezos-mom-single-teen-184512984.html.

18. Genghis X. Shakhan, "The TV, the President, and Twitter Lied to Us About Black Dads," *Shakhan & Wilkerson Law* (blog), February 15, 2021, https://www.shakhanandwilkersonlaw.com/post/the-tv-the-president-and-twitter-lied-to-us-about-black-dads.

19. Julie Bosman, "Obama on Family," *The New York Times*, June 16, 2008, https://www.nytimes.com/2008/06/16/us/politics/15cnd-obama.html.

20. "Letters: JD Vance's Views Against Divorce, Same-Sex Marriage Dangerous," *The Dispatch*, September 8, 2022, https://www.dispatch.com/story/opinion/letters/2022/09/08/letters-jd-vances-views-against-divorce-same-sex-marriage-dangerous/65742847007/; Haley Be-Miller, "Ohio Senate Race: JD Vance Focuses on Conservative Family Issues," *The Dispatch*, August 24, 2022, https://www.dispatch.com/story/news/politics/elections/2022/08/24/ohio-senate-race-j-d-vance-focuses-on-conservative-family-issues/10204420002/.

21. Melissa Kearney, "Marriage, Two-Parent Households, and Socioeconomic Consequences," *The Atlantic*, September 18, 2023, https://www.theatlantic.com/ideas/archive/2023/09/marriage-two-parent-households-socioeconomic-consequences/675333/.

22. Christina Cross, "The Two-Parent Family," *The New York Times*, December 9, 2019, https://www.nytimes.com/2019/12/09/opinion/two-parent-family.html.

23. "The Two-Parent Privilege with Melissa Kearney," Niskanen Center, October 6, 2023, https://www.niskanencenter.org/the-two-parent-privilege-with-melissa-kearney/.

24. Richard V. Reeves, and Eleanor Krause, "Cohabiting Parents Differ from Married Ones in Three Big Ways," Brookings Institution, April 5, 2017, https://www.brookings.edu/articles/cohabiting-parents-differ-from-married-ones-in-three-big-ways/.

25. Mary Parke, "Public Resources and Publications," CLASP, 2003, https://www.clasp.org/sites/default/files/public/resources-and-publications/states/0086.pdf.

26. "The Two-Parent Privilege with Melissa Kearney," Niskanen Center, October 6, 2023, https://www.niskanencenter.org/the-two-parent-privilege-with-melissa-kearney/.

27. Jonah Goldberg, and Brad Wilcox, "There's Something About Marriage," *Tape-Search*, February 22, 2024, https://www.tapesearch.com/episode/there-s-something-about-marriage/XbLF4JRiRmiicwqsDsQcGd.

28. W. Bradford Wilcox, "Suffer the Little Children: Cohabitation and the Abuse of America's Children," *The Public Discourse*, April 22, 2011, https://www.thepublicdiscourse.com/2011/04/3181/.

29. Brad Wilcox, "Elitism, Marriage Rates, and Hypocrisy," *The Atlantic*, February 13, 2024, https://www.theatlantic.com/ideas/archive/2024/02/elitism-marriage-rates-hypocrisy/677401/.

30. William Bennett, "Stronger Families, Stronger Societies," *The New York Times*, April 24, 2012, https://www.nytimes.com/roomfordebate/2012/04/24/are-family-values-outdated/stronger-families-stronger-societies.

31. Jonah Goldberg, "Helping Middle-Class Families," From the Home Front, Jun 27, 2014, https://fromthehomefront.org/?p=1443.

32. James Pethokoukis, "Is Helping Middle-Class Families Social Engineering?," American Enterprise Institute, June 20, 2014, https://www.aei.org/economics/is-helping-middle-class-families-social-engineering/.

33. Brad Wilcox, Robert I. Lerman, and Joseph Price, "Strong Families, Prosperous States," American Enterprise Institute, October 19, 2015, https://www.aei.org/research-products/report/strong-families-prosperous-states/.

34. Jim Tankersley, "Why States with More Marriages Are Richer States," *The Washington Post*, October 20, 2015, https://www.washingtonpost.com/news/wonk/wp/2015/10/20/why-states-with-more-marriages-are-richer-states/.

35. David Brooks, "The Nuclear Family Was a Mistake," *The Atlantic*, March 2020,

https://www.theatlantic.com/magazine/archive/2020/03/the-nuclear-family
-was-a-mistake/605536/.

36. Jonah Goldberg, and Brad Wilcox, "There's Something About Marriage," Apple Podcasts, 2022, https://podcasts.apple.com/us/podcast/theres-something-about-mar riage/id1291144720?i=1000646366093.

37. Willis Krumholz, "Family Breakdown and America's Welfare System," *Institute for Family Studies* (blog), October 7, 2019, https://ifstudies.org/blog/family-break down-and-americas-welfare-system.

38. Jim Dalrymple II, "One Family-Friendly Solution to Our Housing Woes," *Institute for Family Studies*. Last modified December 19, 2023. https://ifstudies.org/blog/one -family-friendly-solution-to-our-housing-woes.

39. ZOLTÁN KOVÁCS, "The Success of Hungary's Family Policy: 2020 Has Been Our Best Year to Date," *About Hungary* (blog), August 13, 2020, https://abouthungary .hu/blog/the-success-of-hungarys-family-policy-2020-has-been-our-best-year-to-date.

40. Ibid.

41. Experiencing a Policy-Induced Baby Boom?," *Institute for Family Studies* (blog), July 10, 2018, https://ifstudies.org/blog/is-hungary-experiencing-a-policy-induced-baby-boom.

42. Daniel Thorpe, "Is Orban's Family Policy Coming Unstuck?," *Spectator*, February 21, 2024, https://www.spectator.co.uk/article/is-orbans-family-policy-coming-unstuck/.

43. P. Polt, "UGYESZSEG, Prosecutor General's Report on Activities of the Prosecution Service in 2019," Prosecutor's Office of Hungary, 2019, https://ugyeszseg.hu/pdf /ogy_besz/ogy_beszamolo_2019_eng.pdf.

44. Anna Sutherland, "How the Military Promotes Racial Equality and Marriage," *Institute for Family Studies* (blog), September 12, 2016, https://ifstudies.org/blog /how-the-military-promotes-racial-equality-and-marriage.

45. Ibid.

46. Rich Morin, "Is Divorce Contagious?," Pew Research Center, October 21, 2013, https://www.pewresearch.org/short-reads/2013/10/21/is-divorce-contagious/; Victoria Richards, "Divorce Is Contagious: Here's Why," *Huffington Post*, November 11, 2019, https://www.huffingtonpost.co.uk/entry/divorce-is-contagious-heres-why_uk_5dce 7840e4b0d2e79f8a9e0e.

47. Jennifer Lundquist, and Zhun Xu, "Reinstitutionalizing Families: Life Course Policy and Marriage in the Military," Wiley Online Library, September 2, 2014, https:// onlinelibrary.wiley.com/doi/abs/10.1111/jomf.12131.

48. Anna Sutherland, "How the Military Promotes Racial Equality and Marriage," *I nstitute for Family Studies* (blog), September 12, 2016, https://ifstudies.org/blog /how-the-military-promotes-racial-equality-and-marriage.

49. Joanna Weiss, "Marriage Political Expert Roundtable," Politico, January 6, 2024, https://www.politico.com/news/magazine/2024/01/06/marriage-political-expert -roundtable-00133856.

50. David Boaz, "Rick Santorum: Limited Government," Cato Institute, December 9, 2009, https://www.cato.org/blog/rick-santorum-limited-government.

51. Jonah Goldberg, "Helping Middle-Class Families," From the Home Front, June 27, 2014, https://fromthehomefront.org/?p=1443.

CHAPTER SEVEN: REVERSE RACISM IS RACISM

1. Michael Harriot, "MLK Is Revered Today but the Real King Would Make White People Uncomfortable," *The Guardian*, January 17, 2022, https://www.theguardian.com/commentisfree/2022/jan/17/mlk-is-revered-today-but-the-real-king-would-make-white-people-uncomfortable.

2. Joshua Bote, "San Francisco to Rename 44 Schools," SFGATE, January 28, 2021, https://www.sfgate.com/education/article/San-Francisco-to-rename-44-schools-washington-15901689.php.

3. Jesse Singal, "Psychology's Racism Measuring Tool Isn't Up to the Job," *The Cut*, 2017, https://www.thecut.com/2017/01/psychologys-racism-measuring-tool-isnt-up-to-the-job.html.

4. Orlando Lugo, "Salesforce Updates Technical Language in Ongoing Effort to Address Implicit Bias," Web Archive, March 17, 2021, https://web.archive.org/web/20230321194237/https:/www.salesforce.com/news/stories/salesforce-updates-technical-language-in-ongoing-effort-to-address-implicit-bias/.

5. Michael B. Rappaport, "Law and Racism," *Notre Dame Law Review* 89, no. 1 (November 2013): https://scholarship.law.nd.edu/cgi/viewcontent.cgi?article=1700&context=ndlr.

6. "Supreme Court Opinions," Supreme Court, https://www.supremecourt.gov/opinions/22pdf/20-1199_hgdj.pdf.

7. "Title II of the Civil Rights Act (Public Accommodations)," U.S. Department of Justice, June 7, 2024, https://www.justice.gov/crt/title-ii-civil-rights-act-public-accommodations.

8. "Harvard Black Students," *The Journal of Blacks in Higher Education*, https://www.jbhe.com/news_views/52_harvard-blackstudents.html.

9. "Students by Country and Level Report 2022–23," Princeton University, 2023, https://davisic.princeton.edu/sites/g/files/toruqf2371/files/documents/students_by_country_and_level_report_2022-23.pdf.

10. Emily Bazelon, and Adam Liptak, "How Will the Supreme Court Rule on Affirmative Action?," *New York Times*, December 8, 2015, https://www.nytimes.com/2015/12/08/magazine/how-will-the-supreme-court-rule-on-affirmative-action.html.

11. Hari Magge, "Princeton Researchers Study How Race Affects Admissions," *The Daily Princetonian*, March 5, 2015, https://www.thedp.com/article/2015/03/princeton-researchers-study-how-race-affects-admissions.

12. Thomas J. Espenshade, Chang Y. Chung, and Joan L. Walling, "Admission Preferences for Minority Students, Athletes, and Legacies at Elite Universities," *Social Science Quarterly* 85, no. 5 (December 2004): 1422–46, https://doi.org/10.1111/j.0038-4941.2004.00284.x.

13. William McGurn, "The Sneaky Road Back to Race Preferences: Will the Supreme Court Stop Anti-Asian Policies?," *Wall Street Journal*, January 22, 2024, https://www.wsj.com/articles/the-sneaky-road-back-to-race-preferences-will-supreme-court-stop-anti-asian-policies-0b9bf6e4.

14. Bernard Mokam, "Affirmative Action Ban and College Essays," *New York Times*, January 20, 2024, https://www.nytimes.com/2024/01/20/us/affirmative-action-ban-college-essays.html.

15. Stewart Baker, "Congress Is Preparing to Restore Quotas in College Admissions," *Reason*, May 15, 2024, https://reason.com/volokh/2024/05/15/congress-is-preparing-to-restore-quotas-in-college-admissions/.
16. "Court Opinion on Diversity, Equity, and Inclusion," *Wall Street Journal*, March 31, 2024, https://www.wsj.com/articles/david-duvall-novant-health-court-opinion-diversity-equity-inclusion-b4a0d50a.
17. Janie Har, "San Francisco Black Reparations," AP News, March 15, 2023, https://apnews.com/article/san-francisco-black-reparations-5-million-36899f7974c751950a8ce0e444f86189.
18. Amy Mayer, "Where Biden Administration's $3 Billion Farming Grant Has Been Going," NPR, January 8, 2024, https://www.npr.org/2023/12/26/1221725620/where-biden-administration-3-billion-farming-grant-has-been-going.
19. "Diverse Supplier Stories," McDonald's, July 22, 2021, https://corporate.mcdonalds.com/corpmcd/our-stories/article/dei-diverse-supplier.html; "Inclusion and Diversity," Starbucks, July 2024, https://stories.starbucks.com/stories/inclusion-diversity/; "Diversity and Inclusion," Disney, https://impact.disney.com/diversity-inclusion/.
20. Aaron Sibarium, "Food and Drug Administration Drives Racial Rationing of COVID Drugs," *Free Beacon*, January 7, 2022, https://freebeacon.com/coronavirus/food-and-drug-administration-drives-racial-rationing-of-covid-drugs/.
21. Ta-Nehisi Coates, "The Case for Reparations," *The Atlantic*, June 2014, https://www.theatlantic.com/magazine/archive/2014/06/the-case-for-reparations/361631/.
22. John McWhorter, "Against Reparations," *New Republic*, July 23, 2001, https://newrepublic.com/article/90734/against-reparations.
23. Mark J. Perry, "Thomas Sowell on Slavery and This Fact: There Are More Slaves Today Than Were Seized From Africa in Four Centuries," American Enterprise Institute, October 18, 2017, https://www.aei.org/carpe-diem/thomas-sowell-on-slavery-and-this-fact-there-are-more-slaves-today-than-were-seized-from-africa-in-four-centuries/.
24. "Masters Theses," University of Massachusetts Boston, 2020, https://scholarworks.umb.edu/masters_theses/661/; Stephen Talty, "White Slaves," Salon, June 15, 2000, https://www.salon.com/2000/06/15/white_slaves/.
25. Laura Italiano, "African American History Museum's Whiteness Exhibit Raising Eyebrows," *New York Post*, July 16, 2020, https://nypost.com/2020/07/16/african-american-history-museums-whiteness-exhibit-raising-eyebrows/.
26. John McWhorter, "Black People Should Stop Caring What White People Think," *The Daily Beast*, July 11, 2015, https://www.thedailybeast.com/articles/2015/07/11/black-people-should-stop-caring-what-white-people-think.
27. Elissa Salamy, "Dad Goes Viral for Anti-CRT Speech: 'I Am Not Oppressed'," KATV, August 23, 2021, https://katv.com/news/nation-world/dad-goes-viral-for-anti-crt-speech-i-am-not-oppressed.
28. Bernadette Hogan, Conor Skelding, and Melissa Klein, "Kids Book 'Our Skin' in NYC Schools Blames Racism on Whites," *New York Post*, May 7, 2022, https://nypost.com/2022/05/07/kids-book-our-skin-in-nyc-schools-blames-racism-on-whites/.
29. Elissa Salamy, "Dad Goes Viral for Anti-CRT Speech: 'I Am Not Oppressed',"

KATV, August 23, 2021, https://katv.com/news/nation-world/dad-goes-viral-for-anti
-crt-speech-i-am-not-oppressed.

30. Jason L. Riley, "In California, the Dream of Racial Preferences Never Dies," *Wall
Street Journal*, May 19, 2020, https://www.wsj.com/articles/in-california-the
-dream-of-racial-preferences-never-dies-11589927296.

31. "Massive increase in Black Americans murdered was result of defund police movement: experts," Fox News, April 19, 2022, https://archive.ph/IMD3K.

32. Jocelyn Grzeszczak, "81% of Black Americans Don't Want Less Police Presence
Despite Protests; Some Want More Cops," *Newsweek*, August 5, 2020, https://www
.newsweek.com/81-black-americans-dont-want-less-police-presence-despite-protests
some-want-more-cops-poll-1523093.

33. Craig Lambert, "Black, White, and Many Shades of Gray," *Harvard Magazine*, May–June
2013, https://www.harvardmagazine.com/2013/04/black-white-and-many-shades-of-gray.

34. Hannah Sparks, "Woke People More Likely to Be Unhappy, Anxious, and Depressed, New Study Suggests," *New York Post*, March 17, 2024, https://nypost.com
/2024/03/17/lifestyle/woke-people-more-likely-to-be-unahppy-anxious-and-de
pressed-new-study-suggests/'; Jared Wadley, "Mentioning White Privilege Increases
Online Polarization," University of Michigan, May 4, 2022, https://news.umich.edu
/mentioning-white-privilege-increases-online-polarization/.

35. "Court Opinions," Court Listener, https://storage.courtlistener.com/recap/gov
.uscourts.paed.610617/gov.uscourts.paed.610617.31.0.pdf.

36. Michelle Goldberg, "Wokeness Is Dying. We Might Miss It," *New York Times*, May
17, 2024, https://www.nytimes.com/2024/05/17/opinion/wokeness-is-dying-we
-might-miss-it.html.

37. "Building an Anti-Racist Vocabulary Podcast: Voting Rights," University of Notre
Dame, November 29, 2023, https://think.nd.edu/building-an-anti-racist-vocabulary
-podcast-voting-rights/.

38. John McWhorter, "Antiracism: Our Flawed New Religion," *The Daily Beast*, July 27,
2015, https://www.thedailybeast.com/antiracism-our-flawed-new-religion.

39. Nikolas Lanum, "Harvard Professor: 'All Hell Broke Loose' When Study Found No Racial Bias in Police Shootings," Fox News, February 16, 2024, https://www.foxnews.com
/media/harvard-professor-all-hell-broke-loose-study-found-no-racial-bias-police-shootings.

CHAPTER EIGHT: *NATIONALISM* ISN'T A BAD WORD

1. Rich Johnson, "Ann Coulter: No Regrets Over Labeling Ramaswamy as 'Indian',"
NewsNation, May 16, 2024, https://www.newsnationnow.com/danabramslive/ann
-coulter-no-regrets-over-indian-label-of-ramaswamy/.

2. Megan Brenan, "Extreme Pride in Being American Remains Near Record Low,"
Gallup, June 29, 2023, https://news.gallup.com/poll/507980/extreme-pride-american
-remains-near-record-low.aspx.

3. "New Study Finds Alarming Lack of Civic Literacy Among Americans," U.S. Cham-
ber of Commerce Foundation, February 12, 2024, https://www.uschamberfounda
tion.org/civics/new-study-finds-alarming-lack-of-civic-literacy-among-americans.

4. "Americans' Civics Knowledge Drops on First Amendment and Branches of Govern-

ment," Annenberg Public Policy Center, September 13, 2022, https://www.annen
bergpublicpolicycenter.org/americans-civics-knowledge-drops-on-first-amendment
-and-branches-of-government/.

5. Jonathan Masters, and Will Merrow, "How Much U.S. Aid is Going to Ukraine?,"
Council on Foreign Relations, May 9, 2024, https://www.cfr.org/article/how-much
-us-aid-going-ukraine.

6. Bethan Moorcraft, "Deceptive Tactic: Nancy Pelosi Disclosed," Yahoo Finance,
January 2, 2024, https://finance.yahoo.com/news/deceptive-tactic-nancy-pelosi-dis
closed-180000159.html.

7. Dom Calicchio, "Dianne Feinstein and 3 Senate Colleagues Sold Off Stocks Before
Coronavirus Crash: Reports," Fox News, March 20, 2020, https://www.foxnews.com
/politics/dianne-feinstein-3-senate-colleagues-sold-off-stocks-before-coronavirus-crash
-reports.

8. Alicia Parlapiano, Adam Playford, and Kate Kelly, "Congress Members' Stock Trading List," *New York Times*, September 13, 2022, https://www.nytimes.com/interac
tive/2022/09/13/us/politics/congress-members-stock-trading-list.html.

9. Ben Wieder, Theo Hockstader, and Amelia Winger, "DC Mayor's Delegation to
China Includes Some Top PAC Contributors," *Miami Herald*, December 6, 2023,
https://www.miamiherald.com/news/politics-government/article281809333.html.

10. Fenit Nirappil, "D.C. Mayor's Delegation to China Includes Some Top PAC Contributors," *The Washington Post*, November 6, 2015, https://www.washingtonpost
.com/local/dc-politics/dc-mayors-delegation-to-china-includes-some-top-pac-contri
butors/2015/11/06/7d1b2a5a-8418-11e5-9afb-0c971f713d0c_story.html.

11. "Closing the Door on FreshPAC," *Washington Post*, November 10, 2015, https://
www.washingtonpost.com/opinions/closing-the-door-on-freshpac/2015/11
/10/875daf08-8727-11e5-9a07-453018f9a0ec_story.html.

12. "5 Facts About Lobbyists," Represent Us, https://represent.us/action/5-facts-lobbyists/.

13. Lee Fang, "When a Congressman Becomes a Lobbyist, He Gets a 1452 Percent Raise
on Average," *The Nation*, March 14, 2012, https://www.thenation.com/article/ar
chive/when-congressman-becomes-lobbyist-he-gets-1452-percent-raise-average/.

CHAPTER NINE: FACTS ARE NOT CONSPIRACIES

1. Eric Lichtblau, "The Reach of War: Arranged Departures - New Details on FBI,"
New York Times, March 27, 2005, https://www.nytimes.com/2005/03/27/washing
ton/world/the-reach-of-war-arranged-departures-new-details-on-fbi.html.

2. Ibid.

3. Joe Silverstein, "Jon Stewart Recounts Angry Backlash Pushing Lab Leak Rant," Fox
News, February 28, 2023, https://www.foxnews.com/media/jon-stewart-recounts
-angry-backlash-pushing-lab-leak-rant-colbert-f-you-done.

4. Jonathan Calvert, and George Arbuthnott, "Inside Wuhan Lab: COVID Pandemic,"
The Times, June 10, 2023, https://www.thetimes.co.uk/article/inside-wuhan-lab-covid
-pandemic-china-america-qhjwwwvm0.

5. Michael R. Gordon, "U.S. Funded Scientist Among Three Chinese Researchers Who Fell
Ill Amid Early COVID-19 Outbreak," *Wall Street Journal*, June 20, 2023, https://www

.wsj.com/articles/u-s-funded-scientist-among-three-chinese-researchers-who-fell-ill-amid
-early-covid-19-outbreak-3f919567?mod=hp_lead_pos11.

6. "TRIP Effectiveness Report," U.S. Department of the Treasury, June 2020, https://home
.treasury.gov/system/files/311/2020-TRIP-Effectiveness-Report.pdf.

7. Chris Cameron, "Jan. 6 Capitol Deaths," *New York Times*, January 5, 2022, https://www
.nytimes.com/2022/01/05/us/politics/jan-6-capitol-deaths.html.

8. Jan Wolfe, "Attack on U.S. Capitol Caused $1.5 Million in Damage, Prosecutors Say,"
Reuters, June 3, 2021, https://www.reuters.com/legal/government/attack-us-capitol
-caused-15-million-damage-prosecutors-say-2021-06-03/; Jennifer A. Kingson, "Riots
Cost Property Damage," Axios, September 16, 2020, https://www.axios.com/2020
/09/16/riots-cost-property-damage.

9. Rebecca Morin, and Matthew Brown, "Harris Compares Jan. 6 to Pearl Harbor
and 9/11," *USA Today*, January 6, 2022, https://www.usatoday.com/story/news/poli
tics/2022/01/06/harris-jan-6-like-pearl-harbor-9-11/9116617002/.

10. Lee Brown, "Biden Calls Capitol Riots 'Worst Attack on Our Democracy Since the
Civil War'," *New York Post*, April 29, 2021, https://nypost.com/2021/04/29/biden
-calls-capitol-riots-worst-attack-on-our-democracy-since-the-civil-war/.

11. Marshall Cohen, "Illinois Removes Trump from Ballot for Insurrectionist Ban,"
CNN, February 28, 2024, https://www.cnn.com/2024/02/28/politics/illinois
-trump-removed-ballot-insurrectionist-ban/index.html.

12. "Capitol Riot FBI Informant," YouTube, https://www.youtube.com/watch?v=pb71O
Jz-5mU.

13. Alan Feuer, and Adam Goldman, "Capitol Riot FBI Informant," *New York Times*,
September 25, 2021, https://www.nytimes.com/2021/09/25/us/politics/capitol
-riot-fbi-informant.html.

14. Alan Feuer, and Adam Goldman, "FBI Informants: Proud Boys," *New York Times*,
November 14, 2022, https://www.nytimes.com/2022/11/14/us/politics/fbi-inform
ants-proud-boys-jan-6.html.

15. Alanna Durkin Richer, "Proud Boys Government Informant," AP News, January 27,
2021, https://apnews.com/article/proud-boys-government-informant-dc84086d78b
688bc585f874452d2b481.

16. "FBI Enlisted Proud Boys Leader to Inform on Antifa," NBC News, March 31,
2021, https://www.nbcnews.com/politics/national-security/fbi-enlisted-proud-boys
-leader-inform-antifa-lawyer-says-n1262578.

17. Alan Feuer, and Adam Goldman, "Oath Keepers Trial January 6," *New York Times*,
November 8, 2022, https://www.nytimes.com/2022/11/08/us/politics/oath-keepers
-trial-january-6.html.

18. Aaron C. Davis, "Warnings of Jan. 6 Insurrection," *Washington Post*, October 31, 2021,
https://www.washingtonpost.com/politics/interactive/2021/warnings-jan-6-insurrection/.

19. "Leaked Audio Exposes FBI Dirty Dealings with Key Informant in Whitmer Kidnapping Plot," Revolver News, March 9, 2024, https://revolver.news/2024/03/leaked-audio
-exposes-fbi-dirty-dealings-with-key-informant-architect-of-whitmer-kidnapping-plot/.

20. "Adam Fox Affidavit," DocumentCloud, https://www.documentcloud.org/docu
ments/7225185-Adam-Fox-affidavit.html; Trevor Aaronson, and Eric L. VanDussen,

"Gretchen Whitmer Kidnapping Informant," *The Intercept*, March 6, 2024, https:// theintercept.com/2024/03/06/gretchen-whitmer-kidnapping-informant/.

21. Ibid.

22. Mitch Smith, "Verdict in Trial for Gretchen Whitmer Kidnapping Plot," *New York Times*, August 23, 2022, https://www.nytimes.com/2022/08/23/us/verdict-trial-gretchen -whitmer-kidnap.html.

23. Mitch Smith, "Jury Acquits 3 Men Accused of Aiding Plot to Kidnap Michigan's Governor," *New York Times*, September 15, 2023, https://www.nytimes.com/2023/09/15 /us/michigan-whitmer-plot-acquittal.html.

24. Trevor Aaronson, and Eric L. VanDussen, "Gretchen Whitmer Kidnapping Inform- ant," *The Intercept*, March 6, 2024, https://theintercept.com/2024/03/06/gretchen -whitmer-kidnapping-informant/.

25. Julie Kelly, "Inside the FBI Tainted Whitmer Kidnap Plot," *The Federalist*, January 19, 2024, https://thefederalist.com/2024/01/19/inside-the-fbi-tainted-whitmer-kidnap -plot-youve-heard-almost-nothing-about/.

26. Joe Barrett, "Trial Over Alleged Gretchen Whitmer Kidnap Plot Likely to Focus on Officials' Activity," Wall Street Journal, March 8, 2022, https://www.wsj.com/articles /trial-over-alleged-gretchen-whitmer-kidnap-plot-likely-to-focus-on-officials-activity -11646735401.

27. "Federal Foreknowledge Jan. 6: Unindicted Co-conspirators Raise Disturbing Ques- tions," Revolver News, June 30, 2022, https://revolver.news/2021/06/federal-fore knowledge-jan-6-unindicted-co-conspirators-raise-disturbing-questions/; "Leaked Audio Exposes FBI Dirty Dealings with Key Informant in Whitmer Kidnapping Plot," Revolver News, March 9, 2024, https://revolver.news/2024/03/leaked-audio-exposes -fbi-dirty-dealings-with-key-informant-architect-of-whitmer-kidnapping-plot/.

28. Ryan Bort, "Jan. 6 Conspiracy Theories: Capitol Riot," *Rolling Stone*, January 6, 2022, https://www.rollingstone.com/politics/politics-news/jan-6-conspiracy-theories-capitol -riot-antifa-1278597/; Steve Benen, "Republicans Aren't Yet Done Concocting Jan. 6 Conspiracy Theories," MSNBC, April 18, 2024, https://www.msnbc.com/rachel-mad dow-show/maddowblog/republicans-arent-yet-done-concocting-jan-6-conspi\acy-the ories-rcna148415; "Bombshell: FBI Agent's Security Clearance Revoked for Sharing Revolver News Article on January 6th," Revolver News, May 18, 2023, https://revolver .news/2023/05/bombshell-fbi-agent-security-clearance-revoked-for-sharing-revolver -news-article-on-january-6th-questioned-allegiance-to-the-united-states/.

29. "U.S. v. Doe," U.S. Court of Appeals for the Ninth Circuit, https://cdn.ca9.uscourts .gov/datastore/opinions/2011/03/21/08-50345.pdf.

30. "United States v. Jones," Justia, https://supreme.justia.com/cases/federal/us/567/709/.

CHAPTER TEN: THE U.S. CONSTITUTION IS THE STRONGEST GUARANTOR OF FREEDOM IN HISTORY

1. Noah Feldman, The Broken Constitution: Lincoln, Slavery, and the Refounding of America, (Macmillan, 2021), https://us.macmillan.com/books/9780374116644/the brokenconstitution.